MASTERING DECISION MAKING

Discover all aspects of making executive decisions including:

- Defining the problem
- Individual vs. group decision making
- The Japanese decision-making style
- Gathering information
- Using creativity in decision making
- Decision making under conditions of uncertainty
- Personal decision making
- Breaking bad decision-making habits
- AND MUCH MORE!

*Don't miss the next book
in the series from the
National Institute of Business
Management*

MASTERING BUSINESS WRITING

THE TOTAL MANAGEMENT PROGRAM FOR THE 1990s!
From the National Institute of Business Management

THIS REMARKABLE NEW SERIES INCLUDES:

MASTERING MEETINGS
MASTERING OFFICE POLITICS
MASTERING DECISION MAKING
MASTERING BUSINESS WRITING
MASTERING BUSINESS STYLE (Coming Soon)

THE ESSENTIAL KEYS TO SUCCESS FOR TODAY'S MANAGERS

MASTERING DECISION MAKING

THE STEP-BY-STEP APPROACH FOR SUCCESS

National Institute of Business Management

BERKLEY BOOKS, NEW YORK

CONTENTS

Chapter 2
Decision-Making Techniques and Tools

Chapter 3
Coming to a Decision

Chapter 4
Personal Decision Making

Chapter 5
Breaking Bad Decision-Making Habits

MASTERING DECISION MAKING

Introduction

Decision making is a significant part of everyone's personal and business life, and making decisions is a distinguishing feature of the management function. But despite the obvious importance and frequency of decision making in business and personal activities, most people still rely on vague and undefined means for making decisions, rather than on any systematic approach.

Decision making is a process. To view it solely as a choice among alternatives is overly simplistic for any problem greater than the choice of what color socks to wear. In the words of management expert Peter Drucker, decision making "can no longer be improvised."

Over the years, there has been a growing awareness, especially within the business community, of the need for the application of a precise step-by-step process when faced with significant decisions. Although mathematical models, computer technology, and various analytic methods have taken decision making into the realms of statistical formulas, probability theories, and computer science, there is no need for a decision maker to become a mathematical wiz.

Decision making can be simple and yet follow a building-block approach, progressing from identifying a problem, to evaluating alternatives, to selecting one of those alternatives. Following a simple and basic plan should lead to more intelligent, reliable, and creative decisions.

The amount of time that business executives must devote to decision making increases as they move up the management ladder. Top executives devote the greatest portion of their time to it. But most people, even professionals, are not taught at any time exactly how to make decisions.

Alfred P. Sloan Jr., after a long career that culminated in heading General Motors, estimated that he would do well if only half of his decisions turned out to be right. Today, if you employ the appropriate decision-making techniques or aids, that batting average can be greatly improved.

The effective decision-making process combines the following steps:

• Defining the problem or diagnosing the situation;

- Gathering relevant information;
- Looking at and analyzing the alternatives and options;
- Comparing and weighing all of the findings;
- Coming to a decision.

Good decision makers carry out each of these steps carefully and completely. Each step has its own factors. If any stage is omitted or executed poorly, the overall process will be marred and the chances of a poor or wrong decision will increase. Employing these basic steps will help you improve the outcomes of your decisions. That certainly is the ultimate reason for developing effective decision-making skills.

The aim of this book is to help you become an effective decision maker in both your personal and professional life.

Chapter One will briefly describe the decision-making process. Chapter Two will detail the various decision-making techniques and tools you can use in implementing the process. Chapter Three explains how to use the information you have obtained to reach your decision. Chapter Four homes in on making personal decisions, and Chapter Five discusses ways to replace bad decision-making habits and attitudes with good ones.

CHAPTER

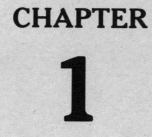

The Decision-Making Process

There are many types of decisions—personal and organizational, major and routine. Each of us makes both major and routine personal decisions that affect our daily activities, our lives, and people associated with us. In our business lives, we generally are called upon to make decisions about our job responsibilities and priorities, as well as decisions that are intended to further the interests of the company.

We are all decision makers and there are many types of decisions

Many managers are able to view their personal and organizational decisions from separate perspectives. Some may even make organizational decisions that contradict their personal beliefs. By identifying actions as being "required by the organization," they are able to make decisions that they could not accept on personal grounds.

For example, a top manager must hire someone for a middle management position. The best candidate is a working mother of two preschool children. Personally, the manager feels she should be more home-oriented than career-oriented, but he extends a job offer because she is the one most qualified and it is the business decision that is in the company's best interest.

On the other hand, there are individuals whose personal interests and decisions are closely tied to those of the organization. They are too personally involved in the business decisions they make and need to resolve the conflicts that occur. Emotions interfere with their decision making.

Major vs. routine decisions

Major and routine decisions are at opposite ends of the pole. Major decisions are individual, one-time decisions involving commitment and, possibly, monetary investment. They usually have a significant impact on one's life or the organization and may be difficult to reverse or change. Thus major decisions should be made thoughtfully and only after thorough, deliberate research. Major decisions could be whether or not to reformulate a product, enter a new market or new product category, open—or close—a plant, change the name of the company, restructure the sales organization, or offer employees a buyout in order to reduce the size of the staff.

Routine decisions, on the other hand, may have a relatively minor effect on one's life or one's company. As a result they can be made more quickly and should not be allowed to take up a disproportionate amount of time. Routine decisions include where to have lunch—and what to order when you get there, which movie to see, how to arrange the furniture in your new office, what to wear to work. An important task for the decision maker, whether he or she is a manager, employee, or individual dealing with a personal matter, is to be able to distinguish the routine from the major and utilize the appropriate decision making approach.

What makes the distinction difficult is that not all decisions can be placed neatly into one category or the other. Many fall somewhere in between. For example, deciding whether to hire an additional assistant or use temporary help is more than routine but less than major. Deciding which telephone message to return first, or which task in your in-basket to handle first, could be routine or it could be something more, depending on who the messages are from or what the tasks involve.

The distinction may also vary from company to company. Equipping the sales force with laptop computers could be almost routine for a financially secure company whose management believes in keeping up with new developments. It could be a major decision for a company in a weaker financial position whose management needs solid proof of the return on investment that could be realized.

Individual vs. Group
Decision Making

History is replete with individuals who rose
to the challenge of making crisis decisions,
but it offers harsher treatment for those
whose decisions went awry. The successful
individuals interpreted the facts correctly,
thoroughly recognized their opportunities,
and, above all, understood the process of decision making.

The one-person decision-making set-up is
in keeping with the popular view of the manager or supervisor. It stems from the small
beginnings of many businesses when one
person made all of the major decisions. As
the business grew, the decision-making process often remained unchanged.

Individual decision making is not archaic
or obsolete. In a crisis or emergency, for example, there may be no time to seek advice
or talk things over with others in a group.
There must be an individual who is capable
of making an appropriate decision without
delay. Sometimes it is best to let the person
who is most qualified make the decision.

However, participative or group decision
making has become a "hot" approach, especially for businesses, as evidenced by the
hundreds of articles that have been written
about it. Today, there is an upsurge of interest in involving employees in thrashing
out solutions to problems via group sessions,

rather than making all decisions at the top and handing them down to the lower ranks. The trend is now toward achieving fuller cooperation at all levels of the organization. In fact, Edward E. Lawler III, a management professor at the business school of the University of Southern California, was quoted in *Fortune* magazine as saying that "maybe 50% to 60% of large corporations use quality circles, problem-solving groups, and other ways to get employee suggestions." U.S. companies have been inspired by the example of the Japanese, whose approach is certainly a marked departure from the traditional top-to-bottom form of hierarchical management.

PROS AND CONS OF GROUP DECISION MAKING

Under certain circumstances, group decisions have been found to have great advantages over individual decisions. The trick is to determine when one method is more appropriate than the other.

The following criteria should be considered when you are faced with the choice between making a decision individually and presenting it to a group for consideration:

What is the nature of the situation? Is the problem one dealing with creativity? Does it require various kinds of information to be brought together or is it limited to one area?

Zero in on the basics before you choose a method

What is the importance of widespread acceptance of and commitment to the solution? Is there a vested interest? If it is vital, group decision making may be considered more readily.

What is the operating effectiveness of the group? Will a quality decision come out of it?

Now let's take a look at the advantages and disadvantages of group decision making. First, what are the *potential benefits* that can be derived from group decision making?

▶ Greater accuracy of decisions. Safety in numbers is the operating theory here. The more individual contributions there are, the better chance there is of coming to the right decision.

▶ Availability of more information. The exchange of knowledge among group members adds up to more than any one person may know and can result in *better* decisions.

▶ Presentation of more alternatives.

▶ Greater acceptance of decisions because more people were involved in making them.

What's involved with a group?

▶ Better cooperation in the implementation of the decision. People who are involved in a decision will execute it better than they will when it is just handed down.

▶ Improved employee communication and better understanding.

▶ Psychological gains. Improved morale, improved motivation, and greater job satisfaction will result from a cooperative effort.

What are the *potential liabilities* of group decision making?

▶ It takes considerably more time. Groups take longer to get together, discuss the situation, and reach a decision.

▶ There can be problems of individual domination.

▶ There can be problems of disagreement.

▶ There can be social pressures on individuals to conform.

▶ There is a tendency to compromise.

▶ There may be indecision. Too much input and too many alternatives may block the way for a clear-cut decision.

▶ There may be participants who have secondary goals and are working for their own purposes.

GUIDING GROUP DECISION MAKING

Following are some key points that will help you guide your group to a sound decision:

• **Include** a balance of talents in your group, according to the kind of decision that is to be made. This may include individuals oriented to long-range and short-range thinking, idealistic and practical thinkers, and mathematical and creative thinkers. Of course, you should be sure to include those whose areas would be significantly affected by the decision.

• **Limit** the size of the group. Any more

13

than six to eight participants is likely to inhibit the effective exchange of ideas. However, in brainstorming, in which the objective is to generate as many ideas as possible, six to twelve participants is ideal. Group size is often dependent on the nature of the decision to be made. For example, when the Allen-Edmonds Shoe Corporation was considering entering a new business, five or six people were involved in reaching a consensus. But if the question involves deciding what kind of advertising to run, two or three people might make the decision.

Pick "neutral" ground • **Hold** the meeting in a room that is on "neutral" ground, not the office of a superior who might be intimidating. The room should be comfortable, attractive, and without distraction.

• **Plan** an agenda carefully and stick to it so that the group does not get sidetracked. But do not be so quick to clamp down on digression that you stifle good ideas.

• **Spell** out any constraints that exist, such as budget limitations, the maximum number of people that can be transferred, and so on.

• **Encourage** open-mindedness and demand that all members listen attentively before responding. To set the proper example, don't rush to criticize offbeat or seemingly "wrong" ideas. If a suggestion does strike you as inappropriate, irrelevant, unworkable, or otherwise troublesome, try to question it in a probing, not a snide, way. For example,

14

asking "How would that work?" could sound like an attack and might intimidate others who fear the same response. A better approach would be to ask, "Could you describe how that would work?"

• **Clarify** any doubts as soon as possible. Although you do not want to squelch others with your questions, you should not hold your tongue simply to avoid stirring things up. If you are confused by something, chances are others are also, and you will help everyone by speaking up. Blame yourself for any gap in understanding by starting your questions with something like "I don't know enough about that area," or, "Am I correct in understanding that...?" Or try "I need something clarified," and then ask your question. It won't be perceived as a criticism, and it will minimize misunderstandings and delays.

• **Control** the incessant talkers. People who strive for personal achievement and recognition may find it confusing and stressful to operate as team players. You can help them—and the group—by both recognizing and limiting their contributions. You might speak directly to the individual: "That sounds like a good possibility, Jane. Let's hear what the others have to say about it." Or address the entire group: "Jane has just suggested that we do thus and such. Does anyone else have any thoughts on that?"

• **Downplay** the self-promotion. Just as you want to keep others from dominating the group, you need to control yourself, too. This can be difficult if you're meeting with several subordinates and want to maintain your position as their leader, or are in a group of your peers and want to shine. But it's important to remember that reaching the best decision is the paramount goal. If you play down your own expertise, you make others feel comfortable about elaborating on their thoughts. And that is the key to getting quality participation from everyone in the group. Another benefit is that the more air time you give participants, the more likely they are to listen to you in turn and to be open to your ideas.

• **Be prepared** to handle any clashes. If the clash occurs during the earlier stages of the process, point out to those who are in disagreement that no decision will be reached until all the information has been presented and all suggestions have been offered; ask them to wait until then and repeat their points. If the disagreement arises when the decision has actually been made, you may have to live with not achieving unanimity. Or, depending on the nature of the disagreement, you may wish to schedule another discussion and ask those who object to the decision to bring in certain additional information.

• **Be suspicious** of agreement that comes too quickly. People may just want to get things over with.

- **Keep** a record of what the group has accomplished and what needs to be done. Assign follow-up tasks if needed and set deadlines for their accomplishment.
- **Call** for an adjournment when agreement can't be reached in one session. Don't let the group settle for a decision that is arrived at through desperation.

THE JAPANESE DECISION-MAKING STYLE

One of the finest and most successful cases for group participative decision making is the Japanese example, which has become a role model for many companies and managers in the United States.

In the Japanese style, the manager must know how subordinates feel about a certain issue in order to maintain the harmony of the group. The manager sees his or her job as that of improving the initiative of the members and creating an atmosphere in which members are continually encouraged and motivated to seek better solutions. Before comparing it with the U.S. style, here is a brief summary of the fundamentals of the Japanese decision-making process:

—It emphasizes taking initiative from the bottom up.

—It makes the manager a facilitator of decision making, not a judge who is handing down decisions.

The Japanese tackle their decisions differently from Americans

—It uses the manager's experience in decision making.

—It pays close attention to the personal welfare of the employees.

An employee who has an idea or a problem prepares an outline called the *ringisho*. The outline is distributed to various supervisors in succession. The objective is to reach a consensus by coordinating the activities of each area that is affected by the problem or idea.

After considerable discussion, a decision is reached and a commitment made by all parties. The manager's status is recognized, but he or she is not burdened with decision making in the Western sense. Each manager assumes that it is his duty to shape decisions by encouraging subordinates to develop the proposal until it has merit and is worthy of being referred to the next manager in the hierarchy. The superiors do not alter the ringisho, but they do assist the originator in improving or altering it, so that a consensus can be reached. The originator also checks the ringisho carefully to make sure nothing in it would offend the superior, thus avoiding conflict.

Everyone in the group is equal

The decision is formulated after all have had their say (as opposed to the Western means, where superiors often make the decision and then try to sell it to the others). The Japanese not only feel that group decision making results in better decisions, but that it is their *obligation* to include the people who will be affected by the decision.

18

Obviously, not every decision can go through such a process. When faced with circumstances requiring a faster or more arbitrary decision, Japanese executives are capable of making it and facing any risks. But they do so with less fanfare. In fact, they might take great pains to explain to subordinates that they didn't like making a decision under such circumstances.

When faced with several alternatives, the Japanese will explore each one in terms of its implementational feasibility. The American drive for an immediate decision, on the other hand, often prompts managers to choose prematurely, perhaps based on conceptual analysis and limited substantive reasoning. Often there is too little concrete examination of how feasible the decision actually is.

The Japanese and Americans both regard experience as important in decision making, but it weighs more heavily in the Japanese style. The Japanese are encouraged to reflect on their experience. Some regularly practice meditation for the purpose of clearing their minds so that they may reflect on their experience more deeply. Many Western managers learn subliminally in this fashion, but they are generally encouraged to get their experience from substantive materials and formal education. The Japanese generally move their managers up through the organization after long experience.

The Japanese don't look to someone to

East vs. West: Differences in management style

"turn things around quickly." The Japanese manager is *there*. He has slowly climbed the ladder and he is not at all burdened by threats to his power or job because he deliberates slowly and carefully. The Western manager would feel more pressure to produce. It is simply less acceptable for an American to "flow" with a situation as the Japanese do.

The accepted American style of decision making is fast, energized, and bold. We admire the "take-charge" person, the one who quips that his or her management philosophy is "Ready, fire, aim." The Japanese image of a good decision maker is the man or woman who is in no hurry to decide until he or she has discerned what really is required.

Many American companies are experimenting with the Japanese style in varying degrees. But it's a change that may not be made easily. American executives who do business with the Japanese sometimes find their approach to decision making hard to deal with at first. One such person is Ronald G. Shaw, who is president of Pilot Corporation of America, the U.S. division of a Tokyo-based company. The first non-Japanese president of a division of this writing-instrument marketer, he has been with Pilot since 1975, when he joined the company as national sales manager.

The "most glaring difference that I have found" between U.S. and Japanese businesses, Shaw says, is that "decisions are made by committees. That's very difficult to get used to." There simply is no such thing as going to one person and asking for a decision, he says. The issue will invariably be discussed and considered at numerous meetings until a consensus is reached.

An attempt to impose such a system upon an entire company might very well cause "culture shock" and meet with some resistance. It could be safer to move gradually and phase in the changes.

However, whether it is an individual decision or a group decision, business or personal, made in the American or Japanese style, all decision makers must follow the appropriate steps in the decision-making process if they want to be effective. Let's now take a detailed look at each of those steps.

Defining the Problem

It has been said that if you ask the right question, your problem will be half solved. The process of correctly identifying and defining a problem or opportunity is the starting point of successful decision making. Unfortunately, perceiving problems clearly is not easy. Too often we apply remedies to what really is a symptom of the problem, rather than to the underlying cause itself. Often, individuals define the decision in

You must say it before you can solve it

terms that are too narrow or restrictive. Making a good decision begins with the stimulus of an accurate question; otherwise, your efforts may lead you down the wrong road.

Begin with the question: What decision must be made?

A careful approach to defining the problem at hand is essential to the whole effort of effective decision making. It begins with the question "What decision must be made here?"

An action-oriented question must be framed, aimed at getting to the root of the problem or opportunity. It must be one that gives direction to the information-gathering activities that will follow as the next step in the decision-making process.

Let's look at some examples where stating the question helps in defining the real problem and leads the decision maker in the right direction.

Assume you have an opening for a supervisor. You have been observing one worker in particular who you feel has the potential to be a good supervisor. If you frame the decision question as, "Should I promote this worker to the supervisory position?" you have already limited the scope of the decision and the number of facts you need to gather. On the other hand, asking the question "How should the responsibilities of this supervisory position be fulfilled?" opens up more options to explore.

The broader question forces you to think about other options that may prove to be more beneficial and more suited to your objective. You might decide to alter the position's range of authority or responsibility, or even eliminate the position as it now stands. Or you may consider alternative candidates for the opening. The point is that if you broaden the question, you will need to acquire more facts and do more thinking about options than if you simply considered one employee for the job. Certainly, it requires more effort on your part, but a better decision is likely to be the result.

The more freewheeling the questions, the better

Take an even larger issue—disposal of waste. The question used to be "Where can we dump it?" with the solution being throwing it into the sea, burning it, or bringing it to vast dumping grounds. But the question was broadened to "What can be done with waste?" This created new options, such as forming landfills, recycling waste, using waste as a source of energy, and many more.

In addition to broadening the question, you must define and phrase the question in terms that make action possible. Suppose, for example, that a manufacturer of gardening tools finds that sales are lagging and profits are declining. To state that a company is losing money is a description of the situation, but it is not an analytical statement of the problem.

What is needed is an action-oriented question such as "How can we strengthen our sales and reverse our profit decline?" As information is gathered, that question may be revised to focus on specific areas that have been revealed as the causes. For example, "How can we defend ourselves against the inroads being made by competitor XYZ in territory 123?"

Building upon the specific question, determine the minimum gains that must occur in order to make a decision acceptable. Also consider the dangers to be avoided and the costs to be contained.

You may encounter difficulties in this phase of decision making. Many a decision maker tends to understate, alter, or skim over unappealing aspects of a situation, especially if they somehow reflect negatively upon the decision maker and his or her abilities. Also, the decision maker's training, background, and personal preferences may affect what he or she perceives. You must minimize personal bias if the situation is to be defined accurately.

Gathering Information

Make no assumptions about where the problem is

Obviously, a decision should not be made unless you are fully aware of the relevant facts. The rule of thumb to observe when gathering facts: *Assume nothing.* Don't make assumptions about where the problem lies or whether you already have all the necessary facts. Find out for yourself or assign your staff to find out. Dissect the problem. Be investigative and analytical. Don't get bogged down in treating the symptoms of a problem; instead, zero in on its causes.

Information is gathered by using search techniques such as observation, reviewing past action, interviews, questionnaires, special reports, checking files and records, and more. There are three major areas to be considered when gathering information: getting the hard facts, consulting with people, and evaluating outside influences.

Getting the hard facts. Following are some possible questions you or your staff should ask yourselves when digging for the facts:

▶ *When was the problem or opportunity first noticed?* Who made the original complaint or suggestion? How was it noticed? Who else is aware of it?

▶ *What events led up to the present situation?* Can a specific factor be pinpointed? Have any recent changes been made that caused it?

▶ *What is the true scope of the problem or opportunity?* Is it really bigger or less important than it may appear to be? Are deeper issues involved? Will a minor adjustment suffice or is a comprehensive, larger solution necessary to resolve the problem or take advantage of the situation?

▶ *Who is affected by the problem?* Is everyone affected or is it confined to one group of people? Is everyone affected in the same manner?

Your mission depends on unearthing the facts

▶ *Is there evidence of any cycles or patterns?* Does the problem or opportunity arise in a given area or at certain times?

▶ *Are there other departments or companies that have encountered this situation?* How do they compare? What have they done?

▶ *What assumptions have been made about the situation?* Are there facts to back them up?

Consulting with people. People contribute greatly to the fact-finding function because the information that is needed may not be documented or recorded and must be obtained by actively seeking it from individuals. Here are some guidelines to follow when contacting people for information:

▶ The investigator should be able to distinguish fact from opinion. Both have a place in decision making, but facts are what you are after at this stage.

▶ Determine what means of questioning best serves the purpose. Some options: formal interviews with prepared questions; informal, conversational questions—either in the office or "on-the-spot"; group sessions where everyone is able to contribute at the same time.

Do what you can to create optimum conditions

▶ Make sure the environment is not inhibiting or distracting.

▶ Make sure interviewers are prepared. Have them plan questions in advance to cover all of the areas about which you need to obtain information.

▶ Explain the reasons for, and goals of, your questioning.

▶ Set aside adequate time.

▶ Take notes or record the conversation for accuracy.

▶ Point out inconsistencies or points that are unclear.

Of course, you are by no means limited to consulting people within your own organization. If you were attempting to answer the sample question posed in the preceding section, "How can we defend ourselves against the inroads being made by competitor XYZ in territory 123?" you would surely want field salespeople to ask customers questions about competitors' activities. If you were test marketing a product or service, it would be imperative to seek input from current customers and end-users, as well as prospects, to determine the viability of the new offering. You might also want to speak to suppliers to find out if they have information on another company's experience in a similar situation.

But it's important to remember here, as in every aspect of decision making, that there are few absolutes. And information, no matter how detailed or persuasive, doesn't guarantee success. For example, General Foods thought it had a winner in its Great Shakes drink mix. In extensive test marketing, all the flavors sold well. But once introduced, the product failed. The reason? The product sold briskly while consumers were trying all the flavors. But they liked none, and eventually stopped buying. The test market had shown that consumers would not only buy the product but would repurchase. Yet it did not reveal that there was a point at which they would stop buying.

Evaluating external influences. When gathering information, there are often external factors such as legal, social, ethical, environmental, and psychological questions that may be relevant to your decision and certainly should be considered. If you feel that any outside factors will be of importance to your decision, include them in your investigation. Remember, however, that gathering information can be made into an endless project. It's important to know when to stop.

Now let's look at how to bring cohesiveness to the facts you have obtained via data (records, files), people, and consideration of the situation. These methods—whether you use one, some, or all of them—will be of assistance as you add facts and proceed with the additional investigation that will lead you to your decision:

Make up a fact sheet. Simply listing the facts as you know them is often the best first step. Make two columns: Label one "Fact" and one "Evidence." You can rank the facts according to importance or certainty. This gives you an array of information in written form and allows you to edit out anything not necessary to the process. The fact sheet also allows you to check the facts against your objectives and determine if any biases or speculations have been included among them. It also may point up any questions to ask yourself or others that may improve the quality of your decision.

Classify your facts into general categories. Break down the facts into categories such as "economic," "human resources," and "marketing," along with "people's opinions." Doing this helps clearly define the areas that may need further investigation or those that are most or least relevant to your decision making.

Use graphics to help you see facts and relationships more clearly. For example, with some personnel problems, an organization chart to point up relationships may be useful. With opportunities involving increased production, a chart depicting past, current and projected figures may point up useful facts and raise questions.

Be creative when arranging the facts

Use polar classifications. Divide the facts into opposite positions such as before and after, for and against, is and is not, or whatever applies to your situation. This works best when the facts appear to be grouped around two positions or ideas.

Set up a list of "data" facts and "people" facts. Compare what your hard data shows with what the people involved told you when you contacted them. This may point up inconsistencies or pinpoint just where the problem or opportunity lies.

Looking at alternatives and options

The solution lies in your choice of alternatives

With the situation defined and the necessary information at hand, it is time for the decision maker to identify and evaluate the possible solutions. Rarely is there only one way to go. There are usually several alternatives or options that might work. Perhaps none is completely satisfactory, so the decision maker looks for more alternatives, hoping to find a better answer.

The search for alternatives often tends to be shortchanged by busy executives because it involves novel ideas and requires some creative thinking. Their preference is usually for clear-cut action along a well-defined or familiar path, so they tend to grasp the first alternative that offers a satisfactory (but not necessarily the best) result.

But identifying alternatives is crucial and invaluable. It is important to acknowledge and write down all the possible alternatives to the situation, no matter how farfetched or unlikely they may seem at first. Only then can you reduce the likelihood that a reasonable alternative was overlooked. Next, the alternatives should be screened to rule out those not pertinent to the situation, and those remaining should be evaluated as possible solutions.

IDENTIFYING YOUR ALTERNATIVES

When you are ready to list your alternatives, you will probably find that the two most common sources of alternatives are (1) the past experiences of the decision maker and the company, and (2) practices followed by other people or other companies. However, don't neglect your own creativity as another source of alternatives. It often adds some new and useful element.

Review experience. The successful action of the past nearly always becomes an alternative for the current situation, if not the front-running candidate. Whether it is a personal decision or a business decision, we are likely to repeat what worked well before, and often it may be the right move. But keep in mind that yesterday's solutions may not be adequate for today's situations; if you open your mind a little more you may find a better solution.

What have others done? While every situation is unique, and different factors are involved in personal and business decisions, relevant alternatives can be gleaned from others. The practice of finding out what others did is a valid source of alternatives if the circumstances are similar.

Studying others can turn up valuable ideas

Much of what businesses call "human research" consists of checking on what other executives and companies are doing. Trade journals and professional papers contain innumerable stories on how companies solved certain problems and made certain decisions. Ideas are exchanged at trade association meetings, through intercompany or interdepartmental visits, or casually by word of mouth. Such information on other companies may produce alternatives that might not occur to executives in your company. On the other hand, keep in mind that even though one company made a decision on a situation similar to yours, it still may not be right for you. Be selective in adopting another company's decision.

Creativity offers opportunity. Every time a person faces a personal or business decision, he or she has the opportunity to be creative. But being creative needn't suggest "far-out" or "blue-sky" choices. It can simply mean originality and uniqueness. Everyday activities are filled with "strains" of creativity: the personnel recruiter who comes up with a creative means of attracting the right job candidates or the clerical worker who comes up with a creative and more efficient means of filing documents. Creativity is within everyone's grasp; it isn't just for stars or something that comes along by chance.

The decision maker should employ ingenuity and creativity in discovering alternatives. Call on others for ideas and suggestions; as mentioned above, a group of people will produce more creative ideas working together than working individually. Brainstorming is one effective means of generating creative alternatives. It can be done on a small or large scale, altered to your needs and for any purpose. It can be done in personal and family situations or for business reasons. Many suggestions may be impractical, but a few may be worth serious consideration.

If you do decide that a brainstorming session is a possibility for putting some creativity into your search for alternatives, keep these basic rules in mind:

Brainstorming is crucial for ingenuity

- Withhold criticism and judgment of ideas until later.
- Welcome the freewheeling and the offbeat. It may be easier to tone down some ideas than to build others up.
- Seek combinations of ideas and try to make improvements on existing ones.

(For more on brainstorming, see p. 33)

Don't try to appraise alternatives as they occur. Withhold judgment during this step. Just lay everything on the table. Of course, there is a practical limit to the number of alternatives that can be identified and some may be readily eliminated because of a lack of practicality, applicability, or funds. But otherwise list all the alternatives before evaluating them.

SCREENING THE ALTERNATIVES

The aim of screening in the decision-making process is to determine which alternatives should be seriously considered for appraisal. You must choose among the various alternatives by eliminating the inferior ones or combining certain elements of others to form a better alternative.

When narrowing down the alternatives, it helps to list the options on paper. While an open mind should be kept, some suggestions might be eliminated fairly quickly because of obvious obstacles. Such factors may be cost, time, manpower requirements, the adequacy of physical facilities, material requirements, and risk.

Weighing your findings

Once you have pared down the alternatives to those that are actually possible and those that may meet your objectives, it is time to evaluate them. This involves weighing the alternatives against your criteria and seeing how they measure up. Here are some factors you should consider:

• What are the potential risks of each alternative? Imagine the decision in operation and list the problems that could arise.

Evaluate the likelihood of these problems arising and what their possible impact would be. Scrutinize the front runner among your alternatives. Sometimes the most likely alternative is quickly adopted and is not examined carefully enough.

How do your alternatives stack up?

• Which alternatives give the greatest results with the least effort? Which alternative will solve the problem or exploit the opportunity with a minimum of disruption?

• How much change would each alternative require? Does it require significant change at once, gradual change, or little or no change?

• Which alternative takes the best advantage of your resources: These include people, equipment, facilities, and the like.

• Would your organizational structure and your managerial and supervisory set-up jell with the alternative?

• How will employees be affected by the alternatives, and how do you think they will react to them?

THE ROLE OF INTUITION

You should also keep in mind that your intuition, gut feelings, and hunches about the alternatives can be very useful in combination with the hard facts. Effective decision makers know that intuition—backed by sound judgment, experience, and intelligence—is a valuable decision-making tool.

One such decision maker is John Stollenwerk, president of the prestigious Allen-Edmonds Shoe Corp. "We started a new business, manufacturing shoe trees, using our gut feelings," says Mr. Stollenwerk. In two years, that business has grown to $3 million. Or course, those gut feelings were well-supported. "We knew the marketplace," he says. "We saw the trends, the prices, and the competition. Also, we've gained historical information just by being in this business for so many years." Still, it was gut feeling that interpreted that information and influenced the decision.

Your own judgment plays an important role

Even before the decision is made, while you are still in the information-gathering phase, your own judgment plays an important role. For example, Zaki Mustafa, general manager of the Serengeti Sunglasses division of Corning, Inc., says that because quantified data "can be twisted any way you like," he prefers to gather data by "asking questions myself." But he cautions that you have to be able to discern the subtext—what people mean, not just what they say. Thus it's important to be able to interpret what you hear.

Intuition is widely perceived as a gift bestowed on the few. Not true. We all have strong intuitive moments when we experience insight without rational thought. But we have been taught to ignore those moments and to favor ideas developed through cognitive reasoning. Logical thinking stands up to public scrutiny in our society, whereas intuition does not.

For example, if you criticize a marketing plan for fact-based reasons and demonstrate an orderly thought process, your opinion will be respected. But if you say, "I just have this feeling it's not going to work," your viewpoint will probably be ignored and may even be scoffed at.

Combined with reasoning, intuition is a source of knowledge that can put you at a great advantage, as the executives mentioned above recognize. If you have been in an environment in which your intuitive thinking has been stifled, there are ways in which you can reactivate it.

• **Don't think in compartments.** For example, if you believe that the only way to approach the problem of declining sales is to do something about your sales staff, you're not tapping into other solutions or approaches. To break through, do some free associating. List all the components of the problem. Next, reel off a list of words as they come to mind. Jot them down as they flow, and review them later to see if any of them point to new directions.

• **Incubate.** The late British economist Graham Wallas, who researched thought processes, found that answers appear suddenly, when least expected. Often, a period of incubation precedes such a breakthrough. To let problems incubate, put them completely out of your mind for a preset time period—hours or days, depending on your deadline. Avoid the temptation to think about them and the answers may occur to you—seemingly from out of the blue.

• **Open yourself to intuitive signals.** Ask yourself, "How does this person, situation, or idea make me feel? What are my emotions trying to communicate to me?"

You'll soon realize that you are receiving much valuable data that you had been ignoring. If you combine reasoning with intuition, you'll be able to weigh the messages from each rather than automatically discounting your instincts. Although you still must demonstrate orderly thought for any decisions aired in public, you can let your intuition influence your choice of options. You'll be able to do what feels right because you'll have a solid basis for the feeling.

VISUALIZING THE ALTERNATIVES

Visual aids put the situation into perspective

In evaluating the alternatives, you may wish to use charts to help you visualize the situation more clearly. Here are some examples that could be altered to suit your situation.

In the chart similar to the one on page 39, for each factor or resource in the left-hand column that is needed for putting the option into effect, put a check in the "need" column. Check the next space whether you have it in

Option: _____				
Factor or Response	Need	Have	Don't Have	Rating
People—number, skills, performance capability				
Time—adequate				
Organizational support—climate, relationships				
Facilities—equipment, space				
Money				
Raw materials				
Knowledge				
External Influences				
Economy				
Competition				
Legal considerations				
Average for this option:				

a form that is usable or just about ready to go. If you need to procure or plan for it, then put a check in the "don't have" column. Finally, assign a feasibility rating, reflecting on a scale of one to 10 your considered opinion as to how much that factor will weigh for or against the option.

For example, if you will require skilled people, that need would be checked. But if those skilled people are already engaged elsewhere in the organization, you would also check "don't have," and that reality would weigh against the option. You may be able to borrow those people, of course, but perhaps not when and for as long as you wish. So your numerical rating might be 0–1. On the other hand, if you need equipment, and it is sitting there waiting for you, your rating might be 10.

Remember that the ratings are subjective, but they can provide you with the beginnings of a selection procedure. They can help ensure that you cover all the necessary factors in your evaluation—and they can also be useful in guiding group discussions.

Another visual aid is the grid below. Here you may evaluate your options according to your criteria with an all-at-once glance. With this grid, set up a rating system, grading each variable A to F or 1–10, or whatever you think will work best for you.

Your Alternatives	Your Criteria					Rating
	Contrib. to Objectives	Cost	Feasibility	Time	Possible Bad Side Effects	
Alternative 1						
2						
3						
4						

EVALUATING THE COST FACTOR

When evaluating the alternatives, getting data on costs is often foremost in the decision maker's mind. Above all factors, cost is most likely to be the least subjective and provides a firm base for most decisions. Alfred R. Oxenfeldt, an author and management consultant who has written a great deal in the area of business decision making, recommends these five steps when estimating decision costs (they may also be applied to many personal decisions):

1. **Describe in detail the action under consideration.** The starting point for estimating and evaluating costs is a specific description of the alternative to be considered. This usually requires information about who

Get a handle on the dollar aspect

would do how much of what, where, with whom, and on what scale.

2. Describe the circumstances under which the action will be taken. This relates to such factors as time, the labor force, materials available, and other circumstances to be taken into account. For example: Are the raw materials needed currently in excess supply and thereby cheaper, or are they difficult to find and expensive? Is it a slow or busy time of year for the electricians whose skills you will need to employ?

Touch all bases when you estimate the costs of your decision

3. Note the effects of the contemplated alternative action on the business. While it is difficult to estimate exactly what consequences will follow from decisions, it is important to try to identify what effects could be likely. An error in estimating is less serious than an error due to entirely overlooked possibilities. Take special care to determine any sacrifices that might result from the contemplated alternative.

4. Assign monetary values to each sacrifice. This step helps the decision maker see the scope of the sacrifice that his or her decision will cause. The computation of a dollar value for something "down the road" or an estimate of intangible sacrifices is difficult to make. There are, however, certain quantitative techniques available (see page 41), especially for decisions in areas of uncertainty.

5. Estimate the impact of the alterna-

Cost Item	Total Costs if Alternative Is Not Implemented	Total Cost if Alternative Is Implemented	Cost of Decision
Raw Materials	$20,000	$25,000	$5,000
Labor	5,000	6,000	1,000
Maintenance	1,500	1,600	100
Administrative Expenses	15,000	15,000	—
			$6,100

tives on the future. Many decisions alter a firm's condition for a long time and thereby affect what it might do in the future and the costs it would incur.

For example, a company may decide to apply its idle resources to a particular use and then find it needs to expand its facilities earlier than it otherwise would have. The decision maker could attach a cost to this effect.

Once you've decided what the decision costs are that are involved, an effective means of getting a good look at your cost situation is to draw up an itemized list of costs and apply them to the alternatives (see chart above).

When it comes to the economics of decision making, sound cost analysis based on the best and most relevant cost estimates available is the best means to a cost-effective decision. It is generally difficult to compute the costs of many alternatives, but those who make the effort will improve their decision-making odds greatly.

CHAPTER

2

Decision-Making Techniques and Tools

Many personal and business decisions can be made simply through your own informal efforts at gathering information, organizing it in your own manner, and evaluating the alternatives. But for complex situations and to increase your chances of making a good decision, there are quantitative tools you can employ as well as creative techniques.

QUANTITATIVE APPROACHES

It is often difficult for the decision maker to juggle and evaluate the pertinent factors involved in a decision and to give each its proper weight, especially within a complex situation or problem. One way to reduce the complexity of the job is to introduce quan-

Quantitative approaches boost your chances for effectiveness

titative analysis tools. These aids range from the listing of pluses and minuses of a contemplated action to the use of elaborate mathematical models and computers. They are playing an increasingly important part in the decision-making process because for most situations, they provide faster and more accurate information. The reason: They simplify reality and reduce complex decisions to a more manageable form. Situations in a variety of business functions as diverse as finance, marketing, production, and personnel have been amenable to quantitative analysis techniques.

The most direct and visible benefits of the quantitative methods are reaped in the projection and analysis of the consequences of the alternatives under consideration. For quantitative techniques to be effective, the situation and objectives must already be clearly defined and the decision criteria selected.

Decision trees

Decision trees are a means of organizing the key elements that go into a decision. They can be drawn to fit all types of situations with any number of alternatives. A decision tree is a visual display of the structure of a situation. It has three components:

▶ Each alternative is displayed as a course of action.

▶ Each course of action has two or more possible outcomes ranging from good to bad.

▶ Each outcome will show an estimated yield or have a numerical value that depends on its probability of occurrence.

A decision tree thus leads you through a series of alternatives with final outcomes shown for each. Here is a simple example: A company wants to bid for a contract to deliver 10,000 cartons of a product. Three possible prices per carton have been contemplated. Each alternative is analyzed in terms of dollar values adjusted according to probability so that an expected value for each bid can be calculated (see chart on page 51). The probability figures that are assigned are based on the opinions of those in the company who are abreast of the market and the competition. In this problem, accuracy is not certain because it is based on subjective estimates. The final column of expected values is calculated by multiplying each payoff by the probability of occurrence. We will assume a $3 direct cost per carton.

Visualize the outcome for each alternative

By using this decision-tree method, the decision maker determines all he or she can about the three options in terms of profits. But he or she must also take into account such factors as how good business is at the moment and whether a brisk business cycle

SAMPLE DECISION TREE

XYZ Company's Contract Bid
(Bid minus direct cost × 10,000)

Decision to Be Made	Alternatives	Possible Outcomes	Dollar Payoff	Probability of Bid Acceptance or Rejection	Expected Value
Which bid to offer for contract of 10,000 cartons	Bid $6.00	Acceptance	$30,000	25%	$ 7,500
		Rejection	None	75%	0
	Bid $5.00	Acceptance	$20,000	50%	$10,000
		Rejection	None	50%	0
	Bid $4.00	Acceptance	$10,000	75%	$ 7,500
		Rejection	None	25%	0

suggests that the high bid is in order, even though the odds are slim, or vice versa.

Decision trees can be designed and refined to fit all kinds of situations. They allow the decision maker to base his or her choice on the most important alternatives and the probable consequences of each.

The matrix

The matrix chart is a flexible means of summarizing the projections the decision maker must weigh among alternatives. Matrices are especially useful as a way to bring the intangibles into focus.

Suppose, for example, that an executive must select a new factory site and has three alternative locations from which to choose. He then identifies four intangible factors that have importance in the decision (availability of labor and skills, favorable union relations, favorable transportation and parking facilities, and the unlikelihood of competition nearby).

Use this method to tackle the intangibles

To arrive at an indication for the significance of the factors at each site, on a scale of 1 to 10, with 10 being the best, he multiplies his rating for the degree of satisfaction expected at each factory site by his rating of how important each intangible is

SAMPLE MATRIX

	Choosing a Factory Site (Projected satisfaction rating × importance rating)				
Possible Sites	Estimated Availability of Labor & Skills	Estimated Favorable Union Relations	Estimated Favorable Transportation and Parking Facilities	Estimated Unlikelihood of Competition Nearby	Total Score
A	7 × 9 = 63	6 × 8 = 48	6 × 8 = 48	3 × 5 = 15	174
B	8 × 9 = 72	8 × 8 = 64	3 × 8 = 24	7 × 5 = 35	195
C	5 × 9 = 45	4 × 8 = 32	7 × 8 = 56	4 × 5 = 20	153

to him and the company (see chart above).

Although the matrix does not make an instant decision for the decision maker, it does force him or her to clarify his or her position on the intangibles and provides a visual means of balancing them in the mind.

All sorts of matrices are possible. You may prefer to use verbal statements instead of numbered ratings or use grades A to F. Probability estimates may also be added. Using the matrix may help you integrate the implications of each alternative into your final decision.

Linear programming

Linear programming is frequently used as an aid to decision making for resource allocation problems. It is an analytical method of finding the optimum combination of limited resources to achieve an objective. Simple allocation decisions often may be made by observation and experience, but in large operations the problems may be complex, involving many options. Linear programming is a shortcut technique that makes possible, in a few hours, solutions that would otherwise take much longer.

Make the most of your analytical abilities

Linear programming is a quantitative method that is usually used with computers because of its complexity. It states problems in the form of algebraic equations in which symbols represent quantities of input. An objective function is minimized or maximized while simultaneously it is made to satisfy various restrictions or constraints placed on the potential solutions. For example, the management of an airline wants to determine how to maximize its profit. However, the operation of the airline is subject to certain constraints: The fleet can consist of no more than 20 planes, 7 of them cannot fly west of the Mississippi River, and so on. Solving the equations in which the problem is expressed yields the optimum combination, as measured by an algebraic statement.

Among the types of allocation problems

that linear programming may help solve are the assignment of salespeople to territories that will result in the highest level of sales performance; how to best allocate supplies, floor space, and labor for the most profit; and the best way to route shipments, to name just a few.

The mathematical techniques that make up linear programming are beyond the scope of this book. But there are some criteria that can help you determine if you could be aided by it:

• The situation is sufficiently complex so that a simple or intuitive decision is not acceptable.

• The situation can be described in quantitative terms.

• The solution will be sufficiently beneficial to warrant the costs of linear programming.

• All the mathematical relationships are linear. That is, they exist only in the first power (not squared or cubed) and if plotted on a graph would yield a straight line.

Models

A model is a means of presenting a situation or condition so that its components may be described, explained, controlled, and predicted. It shows how the various components interrelate.

Models can take on any form that is illuminating to the user and helps him or her reach a decision. A model need not be physical or quantitative. It can also be conceptual. Such intangibles as customer preference, time limits, and job satisfaction may all be parts of a model. Models are flexible and may be constructed to represent your particular situation and the reality of your problem in a manageable way.

Models are important for business decisions

The use of physical models is a common practice in industry. They are representations of the real thing, whether it is a scale model of a plant layout or a small aircraft for testing in a wind tunnel. Needless to say, expense is a factor in these cases, especially if several alternative models are to be built. But it often is sufficient for models to be laid out on the drawing board without doing any actual construction.

Other models, however, assume a mathematical form, consisting of equations relating to variables important to the desired outcome. Some of these mathematical models may be precise and used in situations of relative certainty, employing such certainties as machine capability, speeds, and time factors. Models may also be used in conditions of uncertainty, where decisions are based on estimates of relevant factors in the problem.

Mathematical models generally fall into

two areas: problem-solving models and optimum-value models.

The problem-solving model is designed to provide likely outcomes from the use of each of the possible alternative strategies. The optimum-value model will reveal the best result that can be expected from available alternative strategies. Through mathematical models, a number of outcomes can be examined to find the one that is most likely to reach the decision maker's goals.

Models can be anything you want...

The term "models" can, of course, cover a broad spectrum of visual aids for decision making. Besides physical replications and mathematical models, the term also covers the more commonly used organization charts, flow diagrams, checklists, and other popular visual aids.

Because a model that adequately illustrates the situation for one person may not do the job for another, assessing the usefulness of a model is extremely subjective. Here are some questions to consider if you are thinking of using some kind of model in your decision making:

...and can help you understand how things work

• Does the model allow you to visualize the situation?

• Can the model be readily understood and applied without much preparation and/or practice?

• Is it flexible enough to incorporate additional variables, if necessary?

- Does it allow for the introduction of elements that may change over time?

Models help the decision maker see and understand how things work, which is essential for making effective decisions.

Simulation

Simulation is a means of using models to compare alternative courses of action and to assess the probable future impact of factors over which you can exert varying degrees of control. The general idea of simulation is to build a simplified version of the reality with which you are dealing and to manipulate it (the model) as though dealing with the reality. Simulation can be achieved in many forms, using actual scale models or mathematical models, and more abstract approaches usually incorporating the use of probability mathematics. When a situation can be set up as a series of mathematical equations, computer simulation is useful. The computer can simulate many months of operations in seconds or minutes and has become a valuable asset in decision making.

Simulation lets you compare your alternatives

The results of simulation often show the effects of various alternatives over a lengthy period of time. They may prove to be considerably different from what would have been predicted by traditional means.

Here is an example of a simple computer simulation. A company is deciding whether to build a new branch store. The decision makers feed in the necessary facts, estimates, and assumptions, and the computer simulates the real situation by combining all the information according to the probability of occurrence of each.

DATA INPUT	COMPUTER	RESULTS
1. Costs of building	Simulates situation, combines all data and probability information	Computer issues printouts of:
2. Costs of expanding old site		1. Balance sheets
		2. Profit-and-loss statements
3. Engineering needs		3. Cost analyses
4. Locations available		4. Rates of return
5. Market forecasts		
6. Economic forecasts		
7. Investment required		

The increasing use of advanced mathematical tools and quantitative techniques is an important aid in certain decision-making situations. Although these techniques and their variations are numerous, we have only touched on a few of the basics. But decision makers should be aware of the uses and limitations of these quantitative techniques and their practical applications. When the information these methods provide and the time they save is combined with the elements of personal judgment, logic, and experience, you are likely to come up with a first-rate decision.

However, managers who have faith in their own experience-based judgment caution against over-reliance on quantitative techniques. "Computer information is just numbers," says Mr. Stollenwerk of Allen-Edmonds, "and there's more to a business than numbers." And in the opinion of Mr. Mustafa of Serengeti, "Numbers usually give you black and white conclusions. A computer can say *yes* or *no,* but it can't say *maybe.*"

Decision support systems (DSS)

Decision support systems (DSS) are computerized systems that are used to help make decisions affecting entire departments, companies or other complex organizations. DSS provides computational and analytical data in situations where it is necessary to combine experience and judgment with computer-supported modeling and data.

This method has something for everyone

59

DSS has been successfully used in such management decision areas as long-range and strategic planning, research and development, new-product development, marketing, mergers and acquisitions, and portfolio management. DSS can be used to solve individual problems as well.

Spreadsheet analysis for an entire department or company, corporate financial modeling, budget planning, long-term investment analysis, and many more applications for decision makers are all within reach with new microcomputer software packages. These DSS programs represent the state of the art in computerized planning and decision-making tools.

At snack food marketer Frito-Lay, a division of PepsiCo Inc., DSS is used to tracking the 14 million snacks sold weekly by a sales force of 10,000 people. The salespeople use handheld computers to transmit sales and inventory data to 200 managers. Writing in the *Wall Street Journal*, Frito-Lay president and CEO Robert H. Beeby explained that in addition to helping management track new products and monitor the performance of employees across the country, DSS contributes to the speed and accuracy of decision making.

In one instance, DSS enabled management to pinpoint the competitive situation in a specific store chain that was responsible for reduced market share of one product in one region. Within two weeks management was able to formulate a response strategy. "Before DSS," wrote Mr. Beeby, "finding such a problem and correcting it took the better part of three months."

There are several different types of DSS. Some may overlap in their applications:

Personal DSS is operated by one individual at a microcomputer, usually to solve one specific problem.

Which decision support systems apply to you?

Group DSS has several people, who usually operate within the same work group or department, sharing the same body of data to help them make their own individual management decisions and solve their own problems.

Organizational DSS is used by a wide variety of executives within an organization to aid in any number of corporate decisions. It relies on data from the company's mainframe computer.

Institutional DSS means that the information in the support system can be used repeatedly, with periodic updating, to solve recurring and similar problems.

Ad hoc DSS refers to a situation where the decision maker wants to solve an individual one-time-only problem, so he or she creates a model to address that situation. The decision maker then discards the model and data because it will no longer be useful.

Examine the details before plunging into DSS

While data processing managers are often the prime instigators in setting up company decision support systems, smaller systems are often developed for and by other managers, who often have little computer expertise. Computer experts claim that an individual with no computer knowledge can use DSS.

In evaluating DSS possibilities, you must look at both your hardware and software needs and consider these questions:

• What kinds of problems would we be addressing with DSS? How quickly do we need answers? How accurate must they be?
• Who will be using DSS?
• What are the capabilities of our current hardware? Can it do the job with DSS?
• How much money has been allocated?
• How much experience with computers have potential DSS users in our company had?
• What is the best way to obtain DSS software (buy off-the-shelf packages, develop our own, hire a DSS specialist or consultant, or a combination)?

The implementation of DSS takes time, and the data must be periodically updated. The frequency of update depends on what the DSS is for and what kind of information is stored in the system. In all cases, however, users should monitor changes in the internal and external environment that might affect the information guiding DSS.

Most companies are still not using DSS as often or as effectively as they should, but the rapid spread of microcomputers is gradually changing that.

For DSS packages, consult your software supplier or Data Sources Software. Data Sources publishes semiannually (June and December) a set of three volumes containing information on thousands of software packages, hardware products, vendors, and service companies. The yearly subscription price of $495 also permits subscribers to use Data Sources' hotline number for verification of any new products and services. Contact: Data Source Software, One Park Avenue, New York, NY 10016, 212-503-4400.

Using creativity in decision making

We have the chance to use a little creativity whenever we are faced with a problem or opportunity that represents a decision-making situation. Studies of the creative process and creative people have shown that creativity is not the exclusive province of a small minority blessed with exceptional ability at birth. All it takes is a reasonable degree of intelligence, some mental effort, and, most probably, some stimulus to start the creative juices flowing. Even such seemingly routine

Creativity knows no bounds: Use it to full advantage

decision-making situations as setting up a display or recruiting new employees present opportunities to apply creativity.

For example, a wholesale bakery owner who needed to hire a new employee read about the plight of Chinese women working under poor conditions in factories in her city. She thought she might be able to help one person escape that situation, and at the same time find her new employee, if she could recruit in the Chinese community. But she did not know the language. However, there was a Chinese woman in a professional group to which she belonged. She explained the job requirements to her Chinese colleague, who wrote an ad and placed it in the community newspaper for her.

DEVELOPING YOUR CREATIVITY

To unlock your creativity, use a flexible approach

Many people are quick to say they're not creative. Not true. Nearly everyone can unlock creative abilities to help solve career and personal problems in fresh, innovative ways. But creativity, like intuition (see page 35), is often stifled because we are trained to follow a systematized approach to a problem.

To unlock your own creativity, it is necessary to try a flexible approach instead. The creative person's hallmark is the ability to adopt different kinds of thinking at different points in the problem-solving process.

To help you get started, try this system of thinking in different ways.

- First, be an **explorer**. Most computer programmers spend their time talking to other programmers, bankers to other bankers, and so on. It's better to get out of your pigeonhole and see what's going on in other fields. Explore ideas from other areas, bring them back to your field, give them a twist, and emerge with something innovative. It may help to give yourself one day each month to get outside your department or field to seek out and borrow ideas. Or try joining a new club, or working with more diverse accounts.
- Next, be an **artist**. If you want to develop an idea that's really going to set your industry on its head or dazzle your superior, you must apply imagination to it. Try spending five percent of your day thinking like an artist, asking "What if?" questions and challenging the commonly perceived rules in your field. Question the old standby, "But we've always done it this way." The rules that worked last year may very well work again this year—but you won't know unless you challenge them.

For example, the electronics buyer for a chain of Midwestern department stores repeatedly proposed that his company start marketing fax machines and other business equipment. About two years ago, after being rebuffed many times, he simply stopped trying. But he recently realized that the market for such equipment had expanded greatly, especially with the growth of home offices. He compiled some very convincing market data and presented it to his manager. This time his proposal was accepted.

• Next, the **judge**. If the idea is going to be any good, you must now shift from the "anything goes" attitude of the artist to the "check out everything" attitude of the judge. Is the timing right? What will your course of action be if the idea fails?

Be cautious here. Being a judge requires balance. If you're too critical, you could discard potentially good ideas. But if you're not critical enough, you might try to implement a lot of impractical or even worthless ideas. Thus you should develop the ability to focus on positives. If you determine that an idea is two-thirds good, look for what can be built upon and improved, rather than discarding the whole thing.

• Finally, the **lawyer**. This may be the most important of the four roles. Like a lawyer, you negotiate and find ways to implement your idea within the rules and conventions of your business or field. Your explorer, artist, and judge stages may take a day or week to come up with an idea, but it may take your lawyer phase six months to pave the way for its implementation.

Once you know what your objective is, find out who will help you and keep away from people who will step on your ideas. Finally, be persistent enough to sell and push your ideas until you ultimately reach your goal.

Keep away from those who step on ideas

CREATIVITY IN BUSINESS SITUATIONS

A number of specific techniques have been developed to help stimulate creativity in the business setting. Some can be used by an individual working alone, but they are generally employed most effectively in "creativity sessions" with two or more persons. These methods are usually suggested by management experts as a means of spinning off ideas, some of which will eventually come to form the basis for viable alternatives from which a decision can be made.

Brainstorming. This is probably the best-known and most common technique for stimulating new ideas. It is a method of free association that encourages a flow of ideas, no matter how out of place or trivial they may seem. It is important that no critical judgments be made early in the process (we mentioned some other brainstorming "rules" on page 32).

Brainstorming sessions are usually concentrated meetings lasting under an hour. Participants should not be told the nature of the problem before the session begins. The session should be carefully recorded to make sure that all ideas can be easily recalled for discussion later. It has been suggested that brainstorming sessions work best on Thursday mornings: people have worked up momentum during the week, and their minds are usually fresher before noon.

Storyboarding. This is a form of brainstorming; it takes its name from the posting of idea notes on boards around the room. The method is deceptively simple.

Prior to an idea meeting, a problem is defined and broken down into subtopics or questions. Bulletin board stations—usually two to five—are placed at different locations in the meeting room. Participants are divided into subgroups, one per station. A facilitator asks the members of each group to read the subproblem at its station and write possible solutions on slips of paper or Post-it™ notes—one idea per note. Members attach the ideas to the bulletin board for group members to see. This sparks additional ideas.

After a few minutes, the facilitator asks the groups to move on to the next bulletin board station and offer ideas for solving the next subproblem. When each group has visited each station, the process is complete.

More than 100 solutions may be generated by a typical group of managers in single hour, according to practitioners of storyboarding.

One of the pitfalls of conventional brainstorming is that there may not be equal participation. But with storyboarding, everyone contributes at least one idea per station.

LensCrafters, a nationwide chain of optical stores, has also used storyboarding successfully to analyze success, rather than a problem. During a time of rapid growth, management wanted to identify the reasons for its success so that if anything ever went wrong, they would know where to focus their recovery efforts. During a storyboarding session, managers were asked to answer questions such as: What makes it exciting to work here? What makes it fun? What makes the place challenging? Successful?

The key, easy-to-read phrases written on cards posted around the meeting room yielded a corporate mission statement, a "vision" of the milestones the company wanted to achieve, and a list of the ten "core values" that would guide its operations.

Analogy. Looking for an analogy or similarity to your situation in totally unrelated areas may provide valuable and unexpected insights. It does take some mental effort to use the creative analogy technique. For example, take an inanimate object from everyday life such as a household appliance that performs a function producing a result similar to what you want to achieve. Let that item serve as your model. Study the item, break it into several parts, and consider how it may suggest an approach to your problem.

Analogies can uncover a goldmine of ideas

It may be more useful to choose an example from nature for your analogy. This use of things in nature, animal or plant life as a starting point for new ideas is called bionics, and it has been used successfully in science and industry. (For example, studying the beetle's eye led to the development of a superior groundspeed indicator for aircraft.)

This technique often works best in a group. The leader should seek analogies to the phenomenon with which the group is concerned. The questions that usually follow are: What do these have in common? How do they differ? Do these similarities and differences suggest anything that will help us in making a decision?

Synectics. This word, derived from the Greek, means putting together ideas and things that do not seem to belong together until after they have been combined. Synectics is usually implemented as a group technique, but the method can be used by an individual. The problem or situation is broken apart and analyzed to "make the strange familiar," according to expert Alfred R. Oxenfeldt, and then to "make the familiar strange." It calls for a determined effort to form a new view of a familiar situation and to see that the individual or group doesn't look at the problem in a traditional way.

See a familiar situation with fresh eyes

These are the steps involved in synectics as a group method:

1. The problem is thoroughly analyzed and objectives are determined. Only after everyone is oriented to the nature of the problem can people seek novel ideas.

2. Analogies are generated by free as-

sociation. It is best if the participants are somewhat familiar with the use of direct and symbolic analogies used in synectics. These analogies may include all types of wild ideas and paradoxes.

3. **Connections between the analogies and the problem are defined.** Extrapolate from each analogy to the problem. Be sensitive to new ideas for approaching your problem or situation that are suggested by the analogies.

4. **The group leader assists in assessing the feasibility of the various analogies.** In this way, the technique differs from brainstorming because the group screens the ideas frequently.

Here is a simple example as it relates to a packaging problem: A food manufacturer is seeking a better way to package his product in order to maintain freshness. Through synectics, a comparison is made to a pair of pants. The pair of pants suggests a variety of closing devices such as zippers, velcro, buttons, snaps, buckles, laces, and the like. Not all of these analogous closing devices are appropriate, of course, but they do permit the decision maker to proceed from the conventional approach to more unpredictable paths.

The Delphi Method. This is another popular means of stimulating creativity and has been widely adopted by decision makers in business. This method is time-consuming, however, and is not appropriate when a fast decision is needed. Here is a description of how the approach works:

Get the creative juices flowing with the Delphi Method

• The group participants are queried on how to solve the problem for which a decision is required.

• The participants ponder the question for as long as a few days and then submit their solutions in writing.

• A summary of the solutions is distributed to all participants, with no one knowing who proposed each solution.

• Each participant is asked to evaluate the other participants' suggestions and to offer additional ones.

• The group leader is responsible for summarizing these solutions. He or she then distributes a summarized list of the solutions to the participants along with the comments. They are asked again if they wish to revise their solutions and make further comments.

• The participants receive a review of these comments, together with solutions to the problem, and again are invited to alter their responses.

• After these revisions and a meshing of the suggested solutions have been completed, a consensus should result from a wide spectrum of creative views.

The Osborn Checklist. This approach was developed by advertising executive Alex F. Osborn as a simple means of opening new possibilities for creative thought. The checklist, which is outlined below, provides a series of questions as stimuli to creative decision making:

- Can this idea or object or situation be put to other use?
- Can it be adapted?
- Can it be modified?
- Should it be magnified?
- Should it be condensed?
- Can it be substituted for something else or can something else be substituted for part of it?
- Could its elements be rearranged?
- Could it be reversed?
- Could it be combined with other things?

Twisting an idea can stimulate creativity

While this approach isn't appropriate in all cases, it can be very useful in developing a similar set of questions that fit the decision-making situations that arise with great frequency.

CHAPTER

3

Coming to a Decision

Whatever means you may have used, at this point in the process you have all the information in front of you, possible consequences evaluated, opinions gathered, and gut feelings identified. Selecting the best alternative from those that have been isolated and appraised is the decisive act. You must now say, "This is it." Before you do, however:

- Remind yourself of your objective.
- Keep company policies in mind.
- Measure your choice against your criteria checklist.
- Take a good hard look at your top choice. This is your last chance to consider what could go wrong with it.
- Make your choice after discussing it with all those involved in helping identify

Now you must make the decision

and examine the alternatives, if you still have time. What is the consensus?

• Have an alternative solution on hand so you can shift gears if things don't work out as planned. As management expert Peter Drucker noted, "A decision without an alternative is a desperate gambler's throw."

Prior to your final decision, there is sometimes an other, often overlooked possibility available to you to decrease your chances for error. It is not feasible in every case, but when possible, *test your decision*.

Implementing your decision on an experimental basis is often the best way to validate it. No matter how thoroughly you have analyzed the situation and examined the possible consequences, there is always the potential for problems.

Take one last shot at weeding out any final problems

Give your decision a trial run for a limited period of time. This lets you see how the decision works and allows you to make any changes you see are necessary. Or try a limited implementation of the decision. Implement it for a portion of your staff or in one department, then compare the results to the remainder.

If you have the luxury of testing your decision, be flexible. Make changes whenever problems arise. Don't throw away your chance to improve your decision before it is fully implemented.

Decision making under conditions of uncertainty

No one can predict exactly what the consequences of his or her actions will be. Every decision involves some degree of uncertainty and the decision maker must recognize this fact and make allowances for it. Some "bad" decisions occasionally turn out well, while other carefully thought-out "good" decisions fare badly because of some unforeseen development. For most business decisions and for many major personal decisions (choosing or changing a job, moving to a new city, buying a house), there are always varying levels of uncertainty.

One thing every decision maker must do is take a look at the outside factors contributing to this uncertainty. For the business executive, these include:

Leave yourself a margin of safety for the unexpected

- The general economic climate.
- Happenings in a particular geographic and/or demographic market.
- The current state of the particular business or industry.
- Pertinent laws, regulations, and pending legislation.
- The likely behavior of people, including customers, colleagues, and competitors.

Then, try making an explicit account of the uncertainties involved and consider the following:

79

- What information would help you the most?
- How can the information about future uncertainty be organized in a way to help you come to a decision?
- Process the gathered information, opinions, logic, and impressions into a format best suited for you, such as a checklist, a chart, a written summary, etc.
- Evaluate how all the factors compare and are likely to affect your alternatives. There are formal means for dealing with uncertainty via probability techniques. But these mathematical and statistical methods require in-depth study before you can implement them successfully.

Remember that uncertainty is a part of any decision. Even after the decision has been made, you may never know if the results obtained were the best you could have achieved. When you have serious doubts about how a decision will work, however, you should attempt to leave yourself some margin of safety for the unexpected.

Sticking to the decision

Once the decision has been reached, there is usually a time gap between deciding and acting. Frequently during this period a frightful specter arises. It is known as *second thoughts*. These may be experienced by the decision maker himself or by others who have been involved in the process. Generally, the others are not really convinced that the decision was the best one possible and they begin to have doubts. You can help cut down on this by following these suggestions:

▶ *Be ready to listen.* People who question a decision may just want an opportunity to talk about their concerns. You may not have to sell them on the rightness of the original decision; skillful questions can help them straighten out their thinking. You can reassure them and encourage them to stick with what has been decided. Above all, keep in mind that reservations about a decision are not necessarily harmful.

Handle doubts with facts, not fear

▶ *Have facts on hand to reinforce the decision.* This will help doubters put their fears to rest. Keep available all the information obtained during the information gathering step.

▶ *Make it clear that you are open to reconsidering a change.* Very often during the final decision-making phase, the idea gets across that once the choice has been made, it will have to stick. Not surprisingly, this later discourages people from bringing their doubts into the open. However, it doesn't discourage covert questions about the wisdom of the choice. These undercurrents can be more harmful to a decision than doubts that are openly expressed.

Sometimes, of course, decisions can't be modified; but many can be altered. There may be sound reasons why the decision is being challenged or questioned. To create a supportive climate for questioning group decisions, one manager successfully introduced the following technique: He asks each participant to fill out a form a few days after the final session. Some sample questions used:

- How confident did you feel at the end of the meeting about the correctness of the decision, on a scale of 1% to 100%?
- How confident do you now feel about the correctness of the decision, on a scale of 1% to 100%?
- If you feel substantially less confident now, what factors have influenced you or what aspects of the decision would you like to see reviewed?

In case of a disparity, the manager talks with the respondent or suggests that he or she talk with others who participated in the decision. The manager then decides whether or not to resume deliberations with the group. Even if the decision is irreversible, some of the questioning and rethinking that follow could improve the quality of decision making in the future.

Another problem that often comes up between the time that the decision is made and when it is actually implemented is a lack of communication and understanding of who is to do what and when. An important part of decision making at this time is to spell out who is responsible for carrying out each part of the decision.

Each person must clearly understand what the objectives, standards, and procedures are, and when they are to be accomplished. As soon as these vital factors have been made clear, take the following steps:

- Make sure there is sufficient understanding of the decision and your orders.
- Get agreement on the extent of each person's responsibility for carrying out the decision.
- Establish standards and subgoals as a warning system, to alert you if things are not going as planned.

Second thoughts are bound to exist in the mind of the individual decision maker as well. In most circumstances, if you have followed all the steps in the decision-making process and have taken into account others' opinions and your own hunches, the final decision is the one to stick with and is probably the right one. Backtracking will offer you only one option—make another decision.

Those taking action must understand their roles

Changing the decision

When conditions change, so may your decision

In the real world, however, decisions do sometimes need to be changed. Perhaps events occurred that could not have been anticipated—there is a strike in a supplier's plant; a key subordinate leaves; money tightens up. If you are determined to stick with your original plan no matter what, says one manager, you're not gutsy, you're foolish.

For example, while the marketing team for Rorer Pharmaceuticals' Maalox antacid was preparing its 1990 marketing plans, chief competitor Mylanta was put up for sale by its owners. Suddenly, the announcement came: Mylanta's new owners would be Johnson & Johnson/Merck Consumer Pharmaceuticals, and the marketing would be handled by the company's McNeil Consumer Products Co., sales force.

Rorer, which aimed to expand distribution of Maalox beyond drugstores and into new retail outlets, had already formulated its strategy. But competitor Mylanta also had previously been sold mainly in drugstores, and there was no doubt that its new owners would work to increase distribution in other retail outlets as well. Thus the two products would be going head to head.

"We tore our plans apart," said the Maalox senior brand manager. But even the new plans were not cast in stone. "We've made our decisions," she said, "but we'll constantly evaluate them."

Rorer management had to change its decisions because of something over which it could not possibly have had any control. A much more delicate problem that sometimes faces managers is how to remedy a decision that has proven to be the wrong one—whether it involves an order to a subordinate, a production schedule, or a sales strategy. The solution would appear to be simple: Admit that the course of action isn't working out and set things straight. Yet this often isn't as easy as it sounds.

Some people find it impossible to admit, even to themselves, that they've made an inappropriate decision because they feel that it reflects badly on their abilities. In speaking of the Japanese technique of making decisions by committee, Mr. Shaw of Pilot Pen explains that "a major reason for the consensus decisions is that if a plan doesn't work, there's no one person who's responsible." There is great interpersonal competition, he says. "The pressure is unbelievable, and to make a decision that could go wrong is a horrible thing." That feeling is not unique to the Japanese.

Another concern is the matter of approach. Managers, after all, are in their positions at least partially because their judgment is valued by their superiors. Consequently, this dilemma presents itself: How can a manager admit to, and correct, a mistaken course of action without undermining the confidence of his or her superiors and subordinates?

Despite the obvious need to correct a strategy that isn't working, the ego is involved. What sometimes happens is that a whole structure of errors is created in the attempt to patch up or cover up the original one. The other likelihood is that indecision may set in. A manager may sit on a problem, ostensibly to "give it some thought." But this tactic merely prolongs the agony and allows the effects of a wrong decision to become more complex.

Thus it is important to acknowledge that decisions are not made for all time, and to view a change of course as a new decision. Such an attitude has several benefits:

• It helps to persuade those who dread changing course that occasional shifts are part of normal operating procedure.

• It allows for correcting or eliminating some of the decisions that are sometimes made under stress.

• It promotes initiative and aggressive decision making by others by indicating that nothing is unchangeable.

Examples of the decision-making process at work

The following are three simple examples of an efficient decision-making process in progress:

Putting the steps to the test

Example #1: Improving Production Figures

Defining the problem. Downtime costs and maintenance figures for the packing operation have risen steadily over the last year. Production figures have declined correspondingly. Absenteeism is increasing and operator morale is low. What needs to be done to get the packing operation on the move in the right direction again?

Gathering information. Records show that the packing machines are 15 years old. Files show the increasing frequency of maintenance and repair, especially over the last few years. Operator complaints and supervisor comments confirm that the old and increasingly inefficient machinery is the cause of the production problem.

Production figures are dropping

Looking at alternatives and options. Management comes up with six alternatives:

1. Wait and see what happens in the next few months or years. In other words, take no action presently.

2. Appeal to employees to work harder.

3. Overhaul all the existing machines.

4. Buy the same or similar renovated machines.

5. Buy similar but new machines.

6. Buy new automated equipment.

Screening and evaluating the alternatives. Alternatives 1 and 2 are eliminated. It is decided that some concrete action must be taken now to correct the problem.

Alternatives 3, 4, 5, and 6 are selected as worthy of evaluation. Each of those alternatives is evaluated through research and analysis. The worth of each is determined in relation to expense, its long-term consequences, and a host of other criteria deemed appropriate by management.

Coming to a decision. Alternative number 6 shows the largest rate of return and is chosen.

Example #2: Changing Jobs

Contemplating a job change

Defining the problem. A woman feels that she is in a "nowhere" job and wants to make a change. She is interviewed by a well-respected company and offered a very good position at a branch office 500 miles away. She is unmarried, but does have relatives and friends in and near the city where she resides. What is her best career move at this time?

Gathering information. The woman finds out all she can about the company, the position—including advancement possibilities—and the area to which she would be moving. She checks employment data and opportunities in her current area. She writes down all her personal feelings about it— whether she wants to leave her friends and/ or family; whether a change like this would be refreshing or a burden.

Looking at alternatives and options. The woman decides to consider four options:

1. Stay put for a while longer and take some time to think about her situation and her feelings.

2. Stay put but actively look for a new job locally.

3. Quit the present job and actively look for another locally.

4. Take the offered job and move.

Screening and evaluating the alternatives. The decision maker here eliminates number 1 because she knows she wants to leave her present job soon because it is making her unhappy. Number 3 is also eliminated because it would be a burden financially and emotionally to be jobless. So alternatives 2 and 4 are the possibilities.

In evaluating the alternatives, the decision maker here lists the pros and cons of staying and moving. In addition to the hard facts, she gets opinions and advice from trusted friends and family. Her personal feelings must be examined as well, because these will most likely be the most important single factor in making the decision.

Coming to a decision. The woman decides on alternative 2, to stay in her present job and actively look for a new position locally. While the new job, company, and even the location were appealing, she felt uncomfortable about leaving her family and friends. She was comfortable in her home and felt intuitively that it was not the right time to move. The facts she gathered indicated that the job market in her field was fairly good and that the possibility of a new job in her present locale was likely.

Example #3: Starting your own business

Defining the problem. A human resources administrator at a well-known corporation is dismissed because of corporate restructuring. He is certain he will find a new position quickly because he has become expert in employee benefit plans, which are currently of great concern to most companies, and because he has a number of years' experience. However, he has read several articles about people who, after being dismissed, start their own businesses and find themselves happier, wealthier, or both. Is starting a new business an option for him?

Gathering information. At industry meetings, the administrator has noticed that representatives of many companies, especially the smaller ones, feel overwhelmed by rising insurance costs and the proliferation of insurance plan options. They find it difficult to choose the plan that is best for both their management and their employees. This is an area in which the administrator definately has some expertise and could serve as a consultant..

He checks an industry directory for names of companies that might be prospects. He lists all the equipment and materials he used in doing his job, estimates the cost of buying them on his own, and tries to determine whether he could physically set up an office in his home or would need to rent office space. He calculates how long his severance settlement will cover his living costs, deducting the amounts needed for the equipment and materials. He considers whether he has the necessary discipline to "manage" himself, if he can handle the uncertainty that is a given in a new venture, and also asks his wife about her concerns.

Gathering facts, weighing motivation

91

Looking at alternatives and options. He determines that there are five options:

1. Seek another corporate job immediately, and dismiss the idea of independence as too risky.

2. Seek another corporate job while continuing to consider the possibilities of establishing his own business.

3. Turn his back totally on corporate life and devote all his energies to establishing a consultancy.

4. Create a business plan with a time limit. If he does not have the strong beginnings of a business at the end of that time, he will seek a corporate job.

5. Put out feelers in both directions, looking for a new job and also for consulting clients.

Screening and evaluating the alternatives. Number 5 is eliminated because he believes that it simply is not possible to take both directions at the same time. Numbers 1 and 2 are eliminated because the information he gathered convinced him that, both financially and emotionally, this is the right time to take the risk. His severance pay will carry him through several months, and his wife is earning a good salary. He and his wife both feel exhilarated by the possibilities, not intimidated by the uncertainty. Thus the focus is on alternatives 3 and 4.

Coming to a decision. Exhilaration is tempered by reality, however. He and his wife agree that if his prospects are not strong at the end of six months, he will need to get a corporate job; otherwise their finances will suffer. Thus number 4 is his choice.

Example #4: Deciding whether to fire an employee

Defining the problem. Bobbie, the receptionist and chief switchboard operator, is very well liked by employees and visitors alike. But she's frequently late and often takes unauthorized long lunch hours. She's been warned a number of times, but hasn't changed her behavior. Has the time come to fire her?

Gathering information. The records show that customers who regularly call the company in midmorning and midafternoon have made a point of telling the customer service manager how much they like Bobbie. She recognizes their voices and greets them by name even before they identify themselves. But there have been many complaints from customers about their inability to reach the company early in the morning. Some have been irate enough to cancel orders. Moreover, Bobbie's lunch hour relief operator is constantly complaining that she's getting behind in her regular work, because Bobbie is so late coming back from lunch. A talk with the relief worker's boss confirms the complaint.

Looking at alternatives.

1. Discuss the problem with Bobbie. Show her in dollars and cents how her behavior is affecting the company. Ask for her commitment to change.

2. Discuss how valuable an employee Bobbie has become. Is the problem one of boredom? Are there personal problems outside the office that she needs to focus on temporarily? If so, have Bobbie agree on a specific time frame in which to rectify the situation and get back on track. If the problem is boredom, agree on an enrichment plan and get a commitment from her to change her behavior by an agreed-upon date.

3. Warn Bobbie again. Tell her that if she doesn't shape up you'll put her on 30 days' notice. If she's late again after that, she'll be dismissed.

4. Tell Bobbie that the next time she's late, she's fired.

Screening and evaluating the alternatives. The decision maker eliminates numbers 3 and 4: Bobbie's been warned so often that she doesn't take warnings seriously. Both 1 and 2 focus on communication with Bobbie. Number 1 might work, but it asks only for Bobbie's commitment, not her input. Number 2 gives her an opportunity for input and pledges the company's support so long as she is willing to change. Given Bobbie's positive personality, and her special rapport with customers, this course of action seems to be worth the effort. But, the company can't afford to alienate any more customers because of her lateness.

Coming to a decision. The decision maker concludes that management may be partly to blame for the problem. Not only has it taken no action on its warnings, but also no one has ever sat down with Bobbie to explain how her behavior is hurting the company and herself. Therefore, he decides on number 2. Since she is a valuable employee when she is there, he'll have a serious discussion with her. He'll also ask her to sign a typed statement that she understands that if the agreed-upon time frame isn't met, she'll be dismissed.

CHAPTER

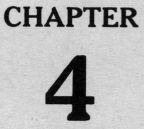

Personal Decision Making

Each day we are faced with countless decisions that shape our lives. Decision making in business is generally acknowledged as a skill. But in your personal life, chances are you think of it as just as routinely as getting dressed, if you think of it at all. Yet good decision making is as important in your personal life as it is in your business life.

Making personal decisions requires skill, too

Throughout your life, you have been making up your mind every day about matters that are minor as well as major, so by now you should have perfected this skill. If that is so, then why do so many people tend to feel anxious when facing decisions? Because most people have developed no method for dealing with the situations that constantly arise that demand some action or decision. The decision-making procedure we have discussed in this book is adaptable and flexible enough to suit many personal situations. But let's take a look at some additional hints that might help you handle personal decisions.

Those seemingly small decisions that we encounter each day may be just as bothersome as the major ones and certainly occur more frequently—what outfit to wear, where to eat out, how to spend the weekend. Though they simply are not as critical and don't call for a long decision-making process, the absence of any kind of process at all puts you in a hit-or-miss situation. This can leave you unhappy with your choice. Here are some suggestions:

▶ Construct a statement in your mind of the results you want from your decision. Be specific.

▶ Set a time limit for your decision and stick to it.

Know what you are trying to accomplish

▶ List the various alternatives and match them against your desired result.

▶ Don't ask for too many additional opinions. Make up your own mind.

▶ Stop when you arrive at something that will give you the results you seek. Little decisions shouldn't be dealt with as life-and-death matters, so exploring every possibility is not necessary.

Facing a critical decision

Even those of us who deal reasonably well with minor decisions often agonize over the critical personal decisions we must occasionally face often cause us to agonize. These are usually decisions that have a significant effect on our lives and often have an impact on others. To test yourself as to how you have fared in the past in your personal decision making—and thereby help yourself analyze where you went wrong or acted correctly—try this exercise:

Think about two or three major decisions that you have made in your life. Try to recall the circumstances and pressures with which you were confronted. Write down each decision and then look over the following list. Try to determine the statement that best reflects the means by which you came to your decision:

_____ I chose the safest way.
_____ I used my intuition and acted solely on my feelings.
_____ I considered all the facts, decided what was important, and anticipated the consequences.
_____ I took someone else's advice.
_____ I did what I thought would be expected of me.
_____ I chose the first option that seemed viable.

How did you do on your last major decision?

_____ I delayed the decision until something came along to decide it for me.

_____ I chose the most difficult option, either for the challenge or for the payoff.

_____ Other.

Now ask yourself:

▶ Did your decision yield the outcome you wanted?

▶ If not, where did you go wrong?

▶ Are you satisfied with the way you made the decision?

▶ What mistakes would you correct and how?

Taking a look at some major decisions from your past and how you handled them will help you determine what your personal decision-making style has been and what areas need improvement.

The next step. When you determine that you are in an important or crucial personal decision-making situation, ask yourself some preliminary questions before getting on with the stages of decision making:

• Why is the decision important to me?

• How might the results of this decision affect my life positively?

Target the decision's impact on your goals

• How might the results of this decision affect my life negatively?

• Will this decision bring me closer to what I want in life? In what ways?

- What obstacles are in the way of my making this decision?
- What kinds of risks, if any, are involved? Are the risks worth it?
- When do I want to take action?

Asking these preliminary questions helps put the scope and importance of your decision-making situation into perspective. Then take a look at yourself and your goals. Often, this will help you take stock of yourself, raise your self-esteem, and help you determine what you bring to the situation. Ask yourself:

- What assets and liabilities do I bring to this situation? Include experience, characteristics, interests, attitudes, and beliefs.
- What personal values do I hold that may be related to this situation? How committed to these values am I?
- What makes me unique?
- What are my goals in life? Include both short-term and long-term goals.
- How does this decision relate to these goals?
- What roadblocks could I encounter on the way to attaining my goals?

Then write a brief goal statement for your decision in answer to this question: *What do I want and how can this decision help me attain my goal?*

You need to know what you want in life before you can make well-informed decisions. Having a good sense of yourself and your goals makes the whole decision process easier; you will probably find you have more going for you than you thought.

The most difficult situations, and the ones most likely to get us into trouble, are those in which we are not aware that we don't know enough. The best thing to do is to remain alert to the possibility that you may need to consult an expert for each major decision you make: You will check with the doctor if you show no improvement in a day or two; you will check with a tax specialist or accountant if you haven't figured out your forms over the weekend; you will check with a realtor about selling the house if you've had no luck by next week.

Acknowledge the need for the advice of experts

Ask yourself at each stage of the decision-making process whether the knowledge of an expert would help you. When you do decide it is time for help in making your decision, ask your most knowledgeable acquaintances for recommendations. If the situation warrants it, seek a second opinion. In this kind of situation, you should take the role of a skeptical decision maker.

What kind of help on personal problems and decisions can be obtained from non-professionals such as relatives and acquaintances? Certainly, where a real professional is needed, he or she should be consulted. But an important point to keep in mind is that even after consulting the best experts, it is still worthwhile to discuss the situation and decision with friends and relatives, regardless of their lack of expertise. Why? Because one of them might alert you to important considerations that you and the professionals may have overlooked, and because they will know you better than the experts. That may be important.

When a decision turns sour

There is no escaping the fact that sometimes your decision will be wrong and lead to an unwanted outcome. But there also is no way that risk can be eliminated from decision making, especially in a decision of major consequence to you.

For example, a young couple took a calculated risk when they bought an older home that they knew hadn't been maintained very well over the preceding year. Although the engineer they called in reported that the house was structurally sound, he did cite some possible problems that would most likely arise within the next few years, although not in the immediate future. Because the couple liked the house more than any other in their price range, they decided to take the risk and buy the house.

Within a year, the basement flooded because of increasingly poor drainage around the house. New electrical wiring had to be put in as well. But even when these risks materialized, this couple, having used sound decision-making procedures, did have some advantages:

▶ They didn't feel guilty or blame themselves for doing something foolish. They had known the risks. People who fail to examine risks often suffer from remorse about their decision.

▶ Having accepted the fact that the risks did materialize, they were more able to decide how to deal with them.

▶ Having been aware of the possible consequences, they had already obtained recommendations from the engineer and from friends as to whom they should contact in case of problems. Thus, they had a head start on handling the negative consequences of their decision.

Effective decision-making procedures will help you determine and assess the risks involved, help you decide what risks you are willing to take, and, most important, help prepare you for the possibility of an unwanted outcome.

Examples of personal decision making

Following are some situations that are fairly common to all of us. They are situations that need to be thought through carefully, and they call for the same decision-making procedure that is used in business situations. It includes these steps:

How the decision-making process is set in motion

- Gathering information.
- Looking at the alternatives.
- Screening and evaluating all the alternatives.
- Coming to a decision.

With each personal decision we will outline the criteria you should consider. There will be some you need not consider in your case or additional criteria that we did not include. But for most of us, the points we list will be important.

Example #1: Buying a home

Defining the problem. A working couple with one child of school age must find a home that will meet their specifications.

Gathering information. The buyers must take stock of such factors as the money available, their requirements in a home, and their preferences. They need to find out about costs and locations, obtain opinions from people in the areas in which they are looking, read up on real estate in those areas, get information from realtors, and continually scan newspaper ads for a "feel" of the market in the areas in which they are interested. They must also get all of the economic information they can about bank rates and the real estate market.

That information might then be arranged as follows:

A. Costs
1. Cost of home
2. Taxes—current and future outlook
3. Upkeep—utilities, maintenance, any foreseeable repairs
4. Homeowner's insurance rates
5. Other—Lawyer fees, broker fees, bank fees, moving costs

B. Location
1. Accessibility—to transportation, work, schools, friends, shopping, recreation
2. School system—reputation
3. Neighborhood—zoning, turnover, demographics, traffic, noise, status

C. Condition of Home
1. Structurally sound
2. Repairs needed—the plumbing, air conditioning, drainage.
3. Cosmetic improvements—landscaping, interior and exterior painting

D. Living Space
1. Adequate number of rooms
2. Closet and storage space
3. Play and entertainment areas

108

4. Layout of house—traffic patterns, stairways
    5. Adequate space for cars
    6. Aesthetically pleasing

E. Other Factors
    1. Status
    2. Property and landscaping
    3. Proximity of neighboring homes
    4. Style of home preferred

Looking at alternatives. The couple has decided to be open-minded and consider several types of housing, several areas, and several styles of homes. They find a realtor for one area and are referred to two other realtors for two other areas within their county. They start their search. They look at townhouse-style condominiums and single-family detached homes.

They are open to all styles of homes from traditional to modern, from small to large, from old to new. They look at homes from the bottom to the top of their price range. In other words, they look at all the feasible alternatives. They also consider the option of waiting another year if they don't find anything they like.

Using the criteria outlined above, they come up with these alternatives:

• A large five-bedroom home, in good condition, with all the aesthetically pleasing elements they want, such as two fireplaces, moldings, old wide-plank oak floors. The price is just right, and the taxes are average. The neighborhood, though by no means bad, does look a bit shabby, with no signs of renewal. The school system, also not bad, is not first rate. But the house itself is appealing and the commute is good.

Rating the available alternatives

• A brand new three-bedroom townhouse condominium in a prosperous community. The cost is less than they had expected. There are amenities such as a pool and tennis courts in the complex. However, there is no land around the house, no room for a garden, and there is less privacy than they wanted. Taxes and schools are good, as is the commute for both spouses.

• A modest home, a bit smaller than they would like but in a very good and prestigious area. The 40-year-old home has some of the amenities, such as a fireplace and well-kept floors, but is rather plain. The schools are excellent, and real estate values are continually going up in the area. The commute is about 15 to 20 minutes longer for both spouses. There is a nice piece of property (with room for expansion). The price is in the middle of their range.

• Just the home they dreamed of in style, size and property, and located in a good community. But it is at the top of their affordability range with high taxes. The schools are tops, the commute shorter, and the status level high. They love it, but recognize that it is a bit steep.

- They can wait and continue looking.

Screening and evaluating the alternatives. Narrowing it down to these options, they apply their criteria to each one. They also use the balance-sheet method, listing the positives and negatives of each option.

Coming to a decision. This couple chooses the third alternative. The home is one they can work with to make it more to their liking and it can be expanded. It is in a good area, which is important because they have a child. Although the price is medium to high, it will not severely hamper them financially. The commute, though longer, is not so long as to disrupt their lives. They decide not to wait because prices are continuing on a rapid rise.

Example #2: Buying a new car

Defining the problem. A woman needs a new car. She needs it to commute approximately 30 miles round trip each day.

Gathering Information. The buyer makes a list of what she wants and needs in a car; how much mileage she will be putting on; what kind of driving she does (highway or local roads). She looks at cars on the road, ads in magazines, reads through magazine articles and rating reports, and browses through dealership lots.

As she does her research, she organizes her findings into these categories:

A. Costs
    1. Price with/without various options
    2. Trade-in on old car
    3. Operating costs—gas and EPA mileage ratings, maintenance requirements (as estimated by consulting services such as *Consumer Reports*)
    4. Insurance
    5. Tax and delivery costs

B. Personal Opinion
    1. Image, status, desirability
    2. Style
    3. Feeling from past ownerships

Comparison criteria for car shopping

C. Accommodation
    1. Roominess—passenger capacity, enough head and leg room
    2. Trunk space—luggage space
    3. Two-door or four-door
    4. Noise level
    5. Satisfactory dashboard

D. Handling
    1. Ease of steering, turning
    2. Responsiveness, acceleration

E. Safety
    1. Crashworthiness ratings
    2. Braking ability ratings

F. Dependability

1. Repair record ratings
2. Parts availability
3. Warranty
4. Reputation of service department

G. Other

1. Availability by certain date
2. Color availability

3. Options

Looking at alternatives. The buyer notes all the automobiles she would like to consider. She visits each dealership, gathering information on the cars according to the criteria listed. She then assembles all the information and makes comparisons. These were the four choices she investigated:

Which alternative is the way to go?

• A modestly priced compact car with good mileage averages and lowest price tag of all, but with reliable ratings.

• A sports car, not excessively expensive, but $3,500 higher than the compact. It is the car of her dreams.

• A mid-sized car, roomy and comfortable for longer trips, safer. The gas mileage is not as good as that of the compact but it's within reason.

• Another modest compact car, with different styling, more to the buyer's liking but with a price tag of $1,500 more.

Screening and evaluating the alternatives. The prospective buyer succeeds in reducing the alternatives down to the two extremes: the lowest price compact or the most expensive "dream" sports car. She decides she will either go all the way for the auto she wants or make the most practical purchase. In other words, she will not compromise on this decision.

Make a list if you have to She draws up a balance sheet to help evaluate the two alternatives. (See opposite.)

Coming to a decision. This choice really comes down to the buyer's head versus her heart. Should she stretch her pocketbook for the sports car and sacrifice in other areas, or pass up the sports car, leaving herself with more money and possibly less financial anxiety? Both cars have good reputations, so that's not the issue. Opting for less financial anxiety, the buyer chooses the compact car.

Example #3: Applying to colleges

Defining the problem. A young man must first choose the colleges to which he should submit applications, then he must choose among the ones to which he has been accepted.

114

SPORTS CAR	COMPACT CAR
1. Dream car	1. Inexpensive—low monthly payments
2. Prestigious	2. Easy to maintain and repair
3. Fun to drive	3. Readily available with choice of color and options
4. Well-made—good reputation	4. Good reputation
5. Good mileage	5. Good mileage
6. Good resale value	

1. Expensive—higher monthly payments than planned, but within budget although stretching it	1. Common car seen on the road all the time (not unique)
2. Hard to repair	2. Not a "fun" car to drive, no prestige
3. Expensive to maintain and insure	3. Low resale value
4. Theft rate high	
5. Takes long to order and deliver	
6. Not much space in it	

Gathering information. When the time arrives for deciding on a college, his parents have already made suggestions and friends have been discussing it endlessly. But though teachers, counselors, friends, and parents can be an enormous help, the young man finds that the real source of information on colleges is the library. It contains copies of college catalogs, numerous college directories, books about college, and magazine articles on the schools. Speaking to alumni or students is also a help, as are trips to likely possibilities that are within a reasonable distance. All of these sources enable the prospective student to get information on the following criteria:

A. Academic Priorities
    1. Accreditation
    2. Degrees offered, courses of study
    3. Admissions requirements
    4. Amount of difficulty in being accepted
    5. Reputation of faculty
    6. Graduate placement record
    7. Advanced, specialized, and technical programs

Get as much information as possible

B. Costs
    1. Tuition, room and board
    2. Books, fees
    3. Transportation

116

C. Funds Available
　　1. Scholarships, grants, and loans
　　2. Work-study programs, student employment opportunities

D. Campus Environment
　　1. Physical setting—city or country, busy or quiet
　　2. Conservative, liberal or mixed atmosphere or reputation
　　3. Variety of campus activities
　　4. Sports emphasis
　　5. Competitiveness—pressure to succeed
　　6. Affiliations—religious, for example
　　7. Proximity to other colleges

What to keep in mind when choosing a college

E. Student Body
　　1. Size
　　2. Coed or single sex
　　3. Faculty-to-student ratio

F. Other Factors
　　1. Prestige
　　2. Nearness to home and friends
　　3. Personal counseling and guidance
　　4. Reputation for particular fields of study

Looking at the alternatives. The prospective college student, using his research, decides to apply to four universities, all of which would require living on campus. (He feels that there is no local school that meets his needs.) The schools chosen vary in size, costs, prestige, location, and ease of admission. All offer sound academic programs and have solid reputations. These are his choices:

• The main campus of his own state university.

• A state university elsewhere but one with a more substantial reputation.

• An Ivy League school.

• A private school that is well recognized but not quite of Ivy League status.

Screening and evaluating the alternatives. This college-bound student has been fortunate and been accepted at alternatives 1, 2, and 4. Now he must set up a system to help him evaluate the alternatives (see chart on page 119).

Another means of evaluating and screening the college alternatives might be to use the matrix method we discussed earlier. Here, he would assign numerical grades to each of the factors, relative to how important they are to him, and add up the totals.

Coming to a decision. Cost is a major factor here, but not the sole one. The decision is made to choose alternative #2, the out-of-state university. The prospective college student feels it offers him what he wants without putting a financial strain on either himself or his family.

Criteria	Alternative #1 Own State Univ.	Alternative #2 Other State Univ.	Alternative #4 Private University
Academic Priorities	1. Sound academic reputation, but nothing outstanding	1. Well-recognized academically	1. Excellent academic reputation
		2. More courses of study	2. Courses of study varied & extensive
		3. Faculty reputation high	3. Fine faculty reputation
		4. Good placement rates	4. High placement record
Costs	1. Least expensive by far	1. Moderate	1. Most expensive
	2. Lowest transportation cost	2. Transportation between school and home expensive	2. Transportation cost midway between alternatives 1& 2
			3. Student employment and/or financial would be necessary
Campus Environment	1. Conservative atmosphere	1. Mixed atmosphere	1. Mixed atmosphere
	2. Beautiful setting	2. Beautiful campus	2. Beautiful campus
	3. Good variety of activities	3. Very large variety of activities	3. Good variety of activities

Criteria	Alternative #1 Own State Univ.	Alternative #2 Other State Univ.	Alternative #4 Private University
	4. Good sports program	4. Excellent sports program	4. Excellent sports program
	5. Pressure and competitiveness level low	5. Fairly high competitiveness level	5. Very high competitiveness level
Student Body	1. Moderate sized—coed	1. Very large—coed	1. Smallest of the 3 alternatives—coed
	2. Faculty-to-student ratio good	2. Fair faculty-to-student ratio	2. Faculty-to-student ratio excellent
	3. Basically students within state	3. Large mix of students from all over country	3. Good mix from all over country
Other Factors	1. Some friends will be attending	1. In an area of the country that interests him	1. High prestige level
	2. Not much prestige attached to this school	2. Fairly prestigious	2. Also in a new area of the country for him
			3. Near grandparents' home

Example #4: Caring for an aging parent

Defining the problem. Three adult siblings must arrange for the care of their elderly widowed mother, who is in failing health. They all live in cities a good distance from her home.

Gathering information. The woman's children seek the advice of her physician, who tells them she must have constant care. Because her eyesight and hearing are failing, and she has become increasingly unsteady on her feet, she could injure herself if left alone. She also is no longer able to drive a car, and therefore cannot shop for herself. Despite occasional memory lapses, however, her mind is still acute, and she is a proud, independent woman.

Her mind is acute, but eyesight is failing

Her children talk with friends who have faced similar situations. They ask for recommendations of nursing homes, senior citizen communities, and in-home care-giving services. They also ask the physician and their mother's clergyman for suggestions. And because the decision cannot be based strictly on facts, but is heavily weighted with emotions, they ask their friends how they feel about the decisions they made regarding their own parents.

They find that in deciding where and how their mother will be cared for, they have these concerns:

121

A. Location

    1. Accessibility for the woman's children

    2. Proximity to medical care

    3. Availability of social activities

B. Safety

    1. Environment in which the woman is less likely to injure herself or be injured

    2. Quality of supervision by caregiver

C. Facilities

    1. Cleanliness—of the building itself and, in nursing homes, of the patients

    2. Attractiveness

    3. Atmosphere—cheerfulness; physical and mental conditions of other residents; attitude of the staff

    4. Recreational activities

D. Cost

    1. Mother's own savings

    2. Children's savings

    3. Insurance coverage

E. Personal feelings

    1. Mother's preference

    2. Children's sensitivity to mother's wishes

    3. Children's concerns for mother's well-being

Looking at alternatives. The children know they must consider having their mother remain in her present home, live with one of them, or move into another residence that can meet her changing needs. To investigate all the options, they research the recommendations they have been given, telephoning the care-giving services and visiting many of the residences and facilities. They eventually come up with these alternatives:

* Her present home. Their mother could remain in surroundings that are familiar and comfortable. The children would hire a live-in care-giver who has nursing training.
* The home of one of her daughters. Both daughters are married. Each works full-time and lives with her spouse in a small apartment that cannot comfortably accommodate her mother and a care-giver.
* The home of her son. He has a spacious home and is well-to-do. He could accommodate his mother and her companion easily. However, his mother and his wife have never had a smooth relationship.
* A nursing home within easy driving distance of both daughters. The facilities are bright and clean, the grounds are spacious, and the staff members appear well trained and efficient. The home was recommended by their mother's clergyman and is affiliated with her faith.
* A garden apartment housing development. Both the buildings and the grounds appear to be well maintained. Because this

is strictly a residential area, with a mix of age groups, there are no special facilities or activities for elderly people. But a community center and shopping center are nearby, as is a hospital with a good reputation. It is much closer to the son's residence, but not unreasonably far from the daughters.

Screening and evaluating the alternatives. The children agree that their mother can no longer remain in her own home, even though that is her preference. There would be no way for them to evaluate the care she would be receiving, nor could they get to her quickly enough in an emergency. Thus the first alternative is rejected.

Weighing the options realistically

They know she will resist moving, however, so they must try to choose an alternative that she will not totally reject. Although she would probably be eager to live with one of her daughters, neither home is a practical choice because of space limitations. Nor is her son's home a good choice, because friction between the woman and her daughter-in-law would create stress for everyone.

All the children are convinced that their mother would get the best possible care in the nursing home. But intuition—"gut feeling"—tells them that she may not yet need this kind of care. She is feeble, but she is not ill, and she values her independence.

The garden apartment is bright and cheerful. Although it is smaller than the house in

which their mother has lived for many years,
they could help her furnish it to her taste. A
full-time care-giver would be hired and the
son, who lives nearby, could visit often to be
sure that all is well. The apartment is quite
costly, however, and that is an expense that
is not covered by insurance.

Coming to a decision. The children decide on the garden apartment. It will be less
disruptive to their mother's life than the
other choices because it will still be her own
home. The son offers to pay a greater share
of the costs because he is better able to do so
than his sisters.

CHAPTER

5

Breaking Bad Decision-Making Habits

Why do so many people have problems making decisions? There are four basic factors that inhibit successful decision making:

Pressure. It often seems as if what needs to be done or decided should have been accomplished yesterday at the latest. There are some emergencies and situations requiring rapid decisions, for example, when jobs and operations are at stake. But it frequently happens that people facing a problem feel disproportionately pressured. Fearful that a delay will only make the situation worse, they rush to make a quick decision, which often turns out to be an unwise one.

We all fall into decision-making traps

Bias. Another factor contributing to an unsuccessful decision is the decision maker's own preference and prejudice. Often because of bias, the decision has already been made in the decision maker's mind, and he or she simply builds a case for it. Prejudice and bias are problems the decision maker must be aware of and overcome to be effective.

Uncertainty. Most people long for order and harmony. They don't like what appears to be floundering, that usually characterizes a decision phase. To get rid of these feelings of discomfort and restore a sense of stability, decision makers often seize the first option.

Logic. Believe it or not, decisions can suffer from too much logic. Most good decisions benefit from creativity and intuition as well as strict rationality.

Some common bad habits and what to do

Procrastination. Excuses such as "I need to think about it" or "We don't have enough information" or "These things take time" are classics. Procrastination is the most common problem in decision making. The procrastinator waits as long as possible and hopes that circumstances will change so that the decision either becomes unnecessary or makes itself.

If you postpone a decision, you can avoid taking a risk and facing the potential consequences. You cannot be responsible for the mistake of choosing the wrong path if you don't choose any path—at least that's the myth. Waiting may also force others to make the decision, thereby *passing the buck*.

Although a certain amount of questioning during the decision-making process is wise, procrastinators tend to indulge in too many "*what ifs*." If you qualify for the title of "procrastinator," try this: Instead of asking "what if," change it to "if I do such and such, the worst that could happen is"—and then carry it to its ultimate absurdity. Psychology tells us that a fear will lose its meaning when carried to absurdity.

But the best cure for procrastination is to impose a time limit. Whether it is a routine decision or a major one, the procrastinator should get into the habit of setting a reasonable time limit and *marking it on the calendar*. Having it written down makes it seem more necessary to make the decision by that date. It is also a liberating action: you know that as of the date you have chosen, you *will* have made the decision and it will no longer be hanging over your head.

Deadlines can cure procrastination

If members of your staff are the procrastinators, you must let them know that you need the decision or solution by a specified date. Overbearing time pressures certainly do not help in the decision-making process. But, as was explained before, a reasonable deadline will help the procrastinator along. Just knowing that there is a deadline, and a time when the decision will be made and you will be free of it, actually helps relieve pressure and encourages him or her to get on with it.

Indecisiveness. People who procrastinate sometimes do so because they are unable to make a decision. But indecisiveness can also manifest itself in just the opposite way: an individual may make the decision, but then keep changing his or her mind. You may have had the experience of seeing an indecisive person drive a restaurant waiter to distraction: "I'll have the filet of sole. No—I think I'd rather have chicken. The special chicken of the day? I'm not sure. Maybe the sole would be better. Or maybe I'll just have a salad . . ." The individual is consumed with fear of making a decision with which he or she will not be satisfied, even in situations where the "wrong" decision would be of little consequence.

An inability to decide can interfere with success

Or consider the comment made by John Feinstein, staff writer for the sports newspaper *The National*, about New York Yankees owner George Steinbrenner, noted for the frequency with which he changes the team's manager: "People talk about how decisive Steinbrenner is. I think he's indecisive—that's why he changes managers all the time."

The inability to reach a decision, and then stick with it unless there is an obvious need to change it, can interfere with an individual's success. It can also make both one's personal and professional life unsettled and unpleasant. But it is possible to teach yourself to make decisions by setting up practice situations.

For example, what should you wear tomorrow? Even if this is a decision you make easily, almost unconsciously, go through the decision-making process just this one time. Define the problem: "I need to decide what to wear tomorrow." Gather information: What your appointments schedule is, what the weather forecast is—whatever you consider relevant. Look at the alternatives: "I could wear the navy pinstripe, the glen plaid, or the light gray." Evaluate each one in terms of the criteria that are important to you. Then, make your choice.

Teach yourself to make decisions

Once you have done this, acknowledge it as a situation in which you have made a decision, and thus have proven that you *can* make a decision.

Create progressively more difficult situations for yourself. When you reach one that really stops you—and you sense your former indecisiveness—set a deadline for making that decision. As of that time you *must* make a decision and stick with it, no matter what. If you are truly dissatisfied after you have made your choice, rethink the decision-making process. And change the decision only if you can find a valid reason for doing so.

Passing the buck. This is another means of avoidance that simply involves turning the decision over to someone else. It is a common practice in many organizations where the buck is often passed in many directions. But it is also common in everyday life, for example, between a husband and wife who keep asking each other: "When should we go on vacation?" Each wants the other to decide, and the one who does will surely get the blame if things go wrong.

Passing the buck is prevalent in situations in which it is not clear who has the responsibility for the decision. It can easily be shifted from one person (or department) to another. Drawing clear lines of decision-making responsibility will in itself save a great deal of time and money wasted every day by buck-passing.

Buck-passers get neither credit nor blame

People who tend to pass the buck might benefit from a new point of view. They should try to realize that if the decision is made by someone else, and things go wrong, it is possible that they could have made the right one and been the "hero." Or if the decision made by someone else was the correct one, they should think "I could have made that decision, too." By passing the buck they avoid any blame, but they also avoid whatever credit goes with making the right decision.

The ostrich syndrome. Another bad decision-making habit is to take the attitude, "It won't happen to me." This often replaces sound judgment and becomes a means of avoiding the need to make a decision. People don't, or rather won't, recognize the signs of an approaching decision-making situation.

They may be given warnings but choose to ignore them. Without any attempt to make an appraisal they conclude that there is no need to worry about a possible problem or the loss of an opportunity. Some examples:

▶ Every day, men and women are warned by their physicians to watch their diet, stop smoking, cut out caffeine, and exercise regularly to lower their risk of heart disease. Rather than begin a healthier life-style, many take the attitude that "It won't happen to me," and continue their unhealthy habits.

▶ A hurricane is approaching and residents of a certain area are told to evacuate and take cover in designated locales. Again, many take the "It won't happen to me" attitude even though there is obvious imminent danger.

Rationalization. Many people fall into this habit by developing and holding onto beliefs that distort information on the basis of what the decision maker wishes the case would be. Rationalization may be prevalent in all stages of decision making and often permits the decision maker the illusion of doing the right thing when in fact he or she is not. Rationalizations have a basis in reality, but usually some key factor is left out or ignored.

Here are a few of the kinds of rationalization we all fall prey to at times:

Another bad habit to avoid: Rationalization

▶ *Denying the bad consequences.* Rather than face up to a bad outcome or disadvantage, we rationalize it and say instead that it's a good one, thereby denying the reality of the situation. For example, "It's a good thing I didn't take that job. I probably wouldn't have liked the kind of work I would have had to do."

▶ *Minimizing the disadvantages.* While not denying any drawbacks, the individual can persuade himself or herself that they are less serious than they really are. "That tiny leak is nothing. It's a great car!"

▶ *Playing up the advantages.* Here the decision maker uses a small gain and overestimates or exaggerates its importance. This often "helps" the decision maker hasten his or her decision.

▶ *Avoiding personal responsibility.* Here the individual blames an outside person or force for a decision. The individual may claim that he or she had no choice, with comments like "The boss made me do it," or "The decision was based on the economic crisis." The decision maker can thus deny any personal responsibility by claiming there was nothing else he or she could do, that his or her hands were tied.

Rationalizations cut deeply into the decision-making process. Yet awareness that you are rationalizing is not easy to come by. You must begin by examining your behavior. Recognizing that you are using avoidance mechanisms is often difficult. But if you are going to be an effective decision maker, it is something that you must correct.

Hastiness. Another bad habit is making the decision too quickly. The consequences of making impulsive decisions may depend somewhat on how intuitive you are. But even if your intuition often serves you well, the impulsive decision is really a means of avoiding the situation, a reaction to tension and anxiety.

Rash decisions can backfire

The decision maker wants to "get it over with." In this case it is a good idea to *write down on paper* the expected consequences of what you decide to do. It may force you to stop and evaluate the options before jumping into a poorly thought-out decision. Of course, the best thing would be to take the decision through the step-by-step process we have outlined.

Quick deciders should remember that rash decisions usually lead to regret. Like most bad habits, rash decision making can be beaten, but it requires a willingness to face the problem and exert the necessary effort.

Overconfidence. Managers often assume they know more than they do. As a result, they may act on insufficient or incorrect information. When that booby trap explodes, it can blow away a career.

Of course, confidence is a business asset that top management prizes highly. It is considered a reflection of competence. Thus confidently expressed opinions may be accepted as fact and not be checked out. Yet prudent

137

managers will double-check both others and themselves, especially on those matters where they feel very secure and confident.

Welcome contradictory advice

It's also wise to search for and even welcome contradictory evidence by seeking other perspectives on a problem before making your decision. If you are in marketing, for example, seek input from people in finance, sales, research, and customer service.

Another useful tactic is to keep statistics on your own track record of decision-making successes and failures. People who neglect to note their success rates tend to delude themselves by remembering only spectacular performances and wiping out all recollection of their blunders. By keeping records, you'll have reminders of the importance of seeking outside help.

Assumptions that hinder decision making

People often make assumptions to avoid the required steps for effective decision making. Certain assumptions are repeated again and again. While there may be a hint of truth to some of them, they are basically generalizations and exaggerations.

Have you ever heard yourself saying any of these things:

"Who knows what will happen in the future? It's a matter of chance, so why go crazy trying to make the best decision?"

Luck and chance are excuses for laziness. Many people feel they are wasting time and effort by working hard to make a decision when the outcome will depend on luck. While luck certainly may play a part in the outcome, and there is no guarantee that your hard work will pay off, your chances of a favorable outcome can be maximized by following good decision-making habits.

"Asking questions is asking for trouble."

A valid decision is based on having enough information and having facts that get at the root of the problem. Asking questions is vital. Yet many decision makers are fearful of probing too deeply and perhaps finding more problems, failures on their part, or other inadequacies they would rather not confront. In fact, any "trouble" that does arise from asking questions in the decision-making process would probably surface eventually anyway and would most likely be in a more advanced state.

"We all agree to the same choice, so it must be the right decision."

Group decision makers often don't want to dissent—to be the odd-person out. Going along with the majority is common in almost every aspect of life. We all desire peer approval and yield to peer pressures. Yet it is especially important to accept varying opinions and disagreements in a group that is appraising alternative courses of action.

"Don't waste your time with nonexperts."

Although getting facts and opinions from experts and professionals may be important to your decision making, don't belittle the value of asking some nonexperts. They may be aware of some facts that an expert isn't. They don't have to be completely right; they just might put you on the track of a worthwhile idea. Seeking information from nonexperts can be useful precisely because they don't have any preconceived ideas about what the alternatives are and may come up with some creative notions that the experts would never have considered.

"If you've asked one expert, you've asked them all."

This is a real cop-out for being lazy and, sometimes, cheap. Most of us recognize that specialists or experts in an area often disagree among themselves. The best thing for a decision maker to do is to find experts who disagree in order to get the different sides of the picture. A typical error is to stick with a single expert's opinion because that is the one with which the decision maker agrees. On the other hand, there are those who will shop around until they find an expert who will tell them what they want to hear. Certainly neither action is advisable, especially in cases where a decision is crucial.

Use experts to uncover differing solutions

"Once the decision is made, that's it, it's irreversible."

A common myth is that once a decision is made it is irreversible. True, once committed it may be difficult and perhaps costly to change your mind. If you discover new evidence that warrants a change of heart, however, it probably pays to alter the decision.

Often, instead of reexamining the problem, people will convince themselves that the commitment is binding and beyond the point of change. This way they don't have to face another decision. However, when a decision does seem to have been a mistake, the consequences of changing it should be closely examined. This examination should reveal in detail what the costs would be both of making a new decision and sticking with the unsatisfactory one you've made.

The role of emotions

You can never completely eliminate emotional considerations

One of the most common illusions about decision making is that it is possible—in business, at least—to squeeze all emotions out of the process. We are all encouraged to make "rational decisions." In reality, you can never completely eliminate emotional considerations when making many types of decisions. And those emotional factors can bias your judgments, even without your being aware of them.

Emotions play a role in every step of the decision-making process. The only question is whether they will help or hurt the final choice of action.

What can you do? You can recognize that these emotional factors are at work, and then develop means of consciously counteracting their effects on the final decision.

This sounds simple. In fact, there are unconscious hurdles that often make it extremely difficult.

Selective perception. The first hurdle you face is "selective perception." In effect, you often see only what you want to see, hear only what you want to hear. Sometimes, when you think you are analyzing a situation "objectively," you are unconsciously asking the question, "Does this situation represent a threat or an opportunity for me?"

If you think of the situation as a threat, you may try to bury it. One frequent evasion technique is to say, "Let's get at the root of the problem." Then, by digging back far enough, you can manage to lose sight of the immediate problem altogether.

On the other hand, if you view the situation as an opportunity, you may leap into it with great enthusiasm, which can blind you to the drawbacks and lead you to underestimate the difficulties.

Selective perception can actually cause you to make a final decision while you are still defining the situation. For example, you may see the situation in such a limited way that all information that might cause you to decide "against yourself" is screened out in advance. Consider the sales manager who believes that only graduate engineers can effectively sell the company's products. If only engineers are interviewed, there is virtually no chance for nonengineers to demonstrate their capability for the job.

One method of minimizing emotions in analyzing a situation is to forget the technical aspects for the moment and try to figure out what the situation means to you. How will it affect your goals? Your status? Now take another look at the situation against this backdrop. Once you realize what effect it has on you—potentially good or bad—you can at least face up to your own emotional pressures.

Another effective technique for overcoming the effects of selective perception is to look at the problem as though it were someone else's—your superior's, your subordinate's, or even that of one of your peers. By trying to sense what emotions would affect their judgment, you may be able to spot parallel factors that are influencing your own thinking without your being aware of them.

Unwritten policies. Another major influence on decision making is company climate. Successful executives are usually knowledgeable about unstated policies that determine how the company is managed. These people may not always realize the extent to which they are affected by top management's attitude toward certain types of decisions and decision makers.

To spot these common, subtle pressures, ask yourself questions like these: Does the company reward risk takers? Does it like to bet on sure things? What is its attitude toward spending money on new equipment or programs? Obviously, such factors can exert a powerful, even if undefined, influence on managers who make key decisions.

Selective assignment. Once you have defined the situation and proceed into the information-gathering stage, another unconscious hurdle usually is at work. Without realizing what you are doing, it is very easy to make a "selective assignment." This means requesting data and assistance from others who are already biased in favor of the decision. If the situation represents a possible "threat," managers may not even ask for needed data, again acting unconsciously.

Finally, when you get information from subordinates, try to spot their biases. How much "sell" is in their reports? What are their motivations? How do those motivations affect the way people conduct research, present findings, and so on?

A point often overlooked is that managers may be giving "unspoken instructions" to subordinates when asking for data. It is easy to say one thing, yet by your attitude indicate another. Note that this can apply up the line as well as down: You must also "read" your own superior correctly. If you don't understand the emotional factors that are affecting him or her, you cannot carry out your assignments effectively.

The consequences. The final step in the decision-making process is turning an idea into action. Here, perhaps, emotions are hardest to ignore. Once you have committed to a decision, you have put your reputation—and your ego—on the line. Can you accept criticism, and then use it or reject it with equal objectivity? If you can, it will help gain acceptance for the decision you reach.

When you are making highly complex decisions, it may be useful to write out a simple five-column table noting briefly the problem or opportunity, the data available, your personal motivations and biases, the emotional biases of others who are involved, and the emotions a decision is likely to engender. A final decision made after such an analysis is more likely to face the real issues than is a decision that is made with assumed objectivity, one that ignores the powerful pressures that emotions can exert.

What does it take to be a good decision maker?

Decision-making demands naturally differ from company to company and individual to individual, but there are some personality factors that usually contribute to decision-making talent. These are not qualities you must possess from birth; they can be developed if you are willing to work at it:

Being a good decision maker takes skill, not luck

Analytical ability. A good decision maker is able to separate a problem into parts, identify and integrate relevant facts, and envision the consequences of a decision.

Conceptual ability and logic. A decision maker must get meaning out of a large array of gathered facts. He or she must pull them together into one concept and see through it all to get to the root of the situation.

Intuitive judgment. Up to a point, the decision maker looks at the situation analytically and logically, but intuition or "hunch" also comes into play. Intuitive judgment is especially important when an immediate decision needs to be made or when all the facts cannot be gathered or are not very clear.

Creativity. A good decision maker encourages new ideas or a fresh approach, recognizing that new or additional material is often necessary for reaching the best decision. A good decision maker, even if he or she is not creative and able to generate original ideas, should recognize and encourage those of others.

Tolerance. A decision maker must be tolerant of ambiguity and frustration and should be able to cope with uncertainties. He or she must also be able to deal continually with difficulties and frustrations without becoming discouraged.

Open-mindedness. A good decision maker makes the effort to listen to others and is also receptive to their comments and suggestions.

Positive self-image. Self-image influences effective decision making in two ways. First, people with a relatively poor self-image often have a greater concern about how they look in the eyes of others and may be unduly sensitive to social pressure. Instead of doing what they believe is right, they may find themselves doing what they think others feel is right. Secondly, individuals with a poor self-image will experience greater anxiety than those with a good self-image. This anxiety may prevent a thorough search for an evaluation of alternatives. Individuals with a poor self-image are less likely to make as effective decisions as individuals with a more positive view of themselves.

Decision-making talent is difficult to pin down, but the above elements have been shown to be present in decision makers with good track records.

A Final Note

Systematic decision making can be hard work, particularly if you're dealing with complicated situations. It's often very tempting to take shortcuts and look for an easy way out. But in the long run, good decision-making tactics and habits will pay dividends in both your personal and business life. If you are willing to take the time and make the effort to follow the decision-making processes that we have presented to you, you will ultimately have a clearer view of the problems and opportunities facing you and what you can or should do about them. Furthermore, you will find that you have greater self-confidence and that those around you who depend on your decisions will have confidence in you as well.

Build self-confidence through logical decision making

The decision-making process almost always requires you to stretch your intellectual abilities, both analytically and creatively. By forming good decision-making habits, you can make that stretch easier and more rewarding.